CoolBrands

An insight into some of Britain's coolest brands 2007/08

superbrands.uk.com

FSC
Certificate No.
CQ–COC–000012

The paper used for this book
has been independently
certified as coming from well-
managed forests and other
controlled sources according
to the rules of the Forest
Stewardship Council.

This book has been printed and bound in Italy by
Printer Trento S.r.l., an FSC accredited company for
printing books on FSC mixed paper in compliance
with the chain of custody and on-products labelling
standards.

2007/08

Chief Executive
Ben Hudson

Brand Liaison Directors
Fiona Maxwell
Annie Richardson
Liz Silvester

PR & Marketing Manager
Hannah Paul

Administrative Co-ordinator
Heidi Smith

Head of Accounts
Will Carnochan

Managing Editor
Angela Cooper

Assistant Editor
Laura Hill

Author
Karen Dugdale

**CoolBrands
Cover Design**
Start Creative

Other publications from Superbrands in the UK:

Superbrands 2007/08
ISBN: 978-0-9554784-1-3

Business Superbrands 2007
ISBN: 978-0-9554784-0-6

To order these books, email
brands@superbrands.uk.com or call
01825 767396.

Published by Superbrands (UK) Ltd.
44 Charlotte Street
London
W1T 2NR

Printed in Italy

ISBN: 978-0-9554784-2-0

Contents

Endorsements

John Noble
Director
British Brands Group

You will find here a compelling display of the wealth and diversity of branding – products and services ranging from clothes to experiences, even to countries. Some cost just a few pounds to enjoy, others are for the super-rich.

Branding contributes to so many aspects of our lives, providing us with fun, confidence, and of course exceptional experiences. This is no happy accident. The organisations behind these brands strive for years, seeking to understand us, investing millions and employing exceptional talent to offer something that continues to excel.

The brands here have achieved formidable reputations but have gone a step further. To be judged a cool brand indicates they are finely in tune with today's culture and mood. The British Brands Group, the voice for brands in the UK, applauds their achievement and continues to work to ensure the best environment for them to continue to deliver their magic.

Derek Holder
Managing Director
The Institute of Direct Marketing

We are extremely pleased to support CoolBrands 2007/08. In the last 5-10 years the branding landscape has changed dramatically with new media, new markets, new channels and new challenges. The profession is not only far more sophisticated but is now more complex and competitive. The IDM applauds initiatives that contribute to greater recognition of branding and in particular those brands that have elevated themselves above their peers in the challenging and fast paced 'cool' brand arena.

The IDM is proud to be involved in the CoolBrands project and hopes that the insights and case studies featured within these covers help to further our understanding of the hard work and discipline required to build a successful 'CoolBrand'.

James Aitchison
Managing Editor
World Advertising Research Center

Those of us who ply our trade in the world of brand marketing are used to grappling with elusive concepts. None come more slippery than 'cool' – that fickle stardust so difficult to win, yet so easy to lose.

But whilst we struggle, like frustrated alchemists, trying to understand and define just what cool is, over recent years Superbrands has arguably done something much more useful – it has shown us where it is. And of course, in doing so, it has aided our understanding of cool immeasurably.

This latest collection of CoolBrands confirms that cool is alive, well and working its magic on brands in all markets, serving all demographics. It also confirms the one thing that cool brands have in common – that intangible extra you can't quite define.

Whilst that remains the case, as I imagine it will, WARC has no hesitation at all in endorsing the CoolBrands programme and welcoming the brand profiles it generates as vital content for WARC.com.

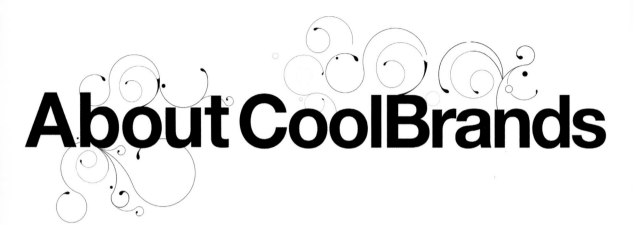

About CoolBrands

The CoolBrands programme was founded by the Superbrands organisation with the aim of paying tribute to the UK's coolest brands, by presenting expert and consumer opinion on the UK's strongest brands in terms of innovation, style and desirability.

The independent and voluntary CoolBrands Council (listed opposite) consists of eminent individuals, well qualified to judge which are the nation's coolest brands. Each brand featured in this publication has qualified based on the opinion of this Council as well as a dedicated consumer election, which is run by YouGov.

A CoolBrand should be stylish, innovative, original, authentic, desirable and unique.

Through identifying these brands and providing their case histories, the organisation hopes that people will gain a deeper appreciation of the discipline of branding and a greater understanding of the brands themselves.

Beyond this publication, the CoolBrands 2007/08 programme has a presence online at www.superbrands.uk.com. In addition, representatives of the Superbrands organisation make frequent appearances on TV and radio, as well as providing comment for newspapers on branding and the nature of cool.

CoolBrands Stamp

The brands that have been awarded CoolBrand status and participate in the programme, are given permission to use the CoolBrands Stamp.

This powerful endorsement provides evidence to existing and potential consumers, the media, employees and investors of the exceptional standing that these CoolBrands have achieved.

Member brands use the stamp on marketing materials such as product packaging, POS items, advertising, websites and annual reports, as well as in conjunction with other external and internal communication channels.

AWARDED FOR
UK
CoolBrands
2007/08
INNOVATION · STYLE · DESIRABILITY

VOTED ONE OF THE UK'S COOLEST BRANDS
BY EXPERTS & CONSUMERS

CoolBrands Council 2007/08

Ralph Ardill
Founder & CEO
The Brand Experience Consultancy

Niku Banaie
Managing Partner
Naked Communications

Damian Barr
Journalist, Writer, Playwright
& Presenter

Nicki Bidder
Editor-in-Chief
Dazed & Confused

Paul Croughton
Assistant Travel Editor
The Sunday Times

Jodie Dalmeda
Media Consultant

Ekow Eshun
Artistic Director
Institute of Contemporary Arts

Lee Farrant
Partner
RPM

Sandra Halliday
Managing Editor
Business Reporting & Analysis
WGSN.com

Andrew Harrison
Associate Editor, The Word
& Editor-in-Chief, Mixmag

Cozmo Jenks
Milliner

Dolly Jones
Editor
VOGUE.COM

Owen Lee &
Gary Robinson
Creative Partners
Farm

Ben de Lisi
Fashion Designer

Meritaten Mance
Co-Founder & Director
Kitchen Communications

Simon Mathews
Founding Partner
Rise Communications

Trevor Nelson
DJ

Vaishaly Patel
A-list Facialist

Bakul Patki
PR, Production & Project Development
in Arts, Entertainment & Media

Mary Portas
Founding Partner & Creative Director
Yellowdoor

Alex Proud
Director
Proud Galleries Ltd

Nicolas Roope
Founding Partner
Poke London

June Sarpong
Presenter

Tom Savigar
Partner
The Future Laboratory

Dylan Williams
Strategy Director
Mother London

Stephen Cheliotis
Chairman
Superbrands Councils UK

CoolBrands Selection Process

Independent researchers use a wide range of sources to compile a list of the UK's leading cool brands. From the thousands of brands initially considered, an extensive list of just under 1,200 brands is forwarded to the CoolBrands Council.

The independent and voluntary council considers the list and members individually award each brand a score from 1-10. The score is intuitive, but Council members are asked to bear in mind how stylish, innovative, original, authentic, desirable and unique each brand is. Council members are not allowed to score brands with which they have a direct association or are in direct competition to. The lowest-scoring 50 per cent of brands are eliminated at this stage.

A nationally representative panel of 3,265 consumers is surveyed by YouGov, the UK's most accurate online research agency. These individuals are asked to vote on the surviving 625 brands which remain after the Council has scored.

The surviving brands are ranked based on the combined score of the CoolBrands Council (70 per cent) and the consumer panel (30 per cent). The lowest-scoring brands are eliminated while the leading 500 brands are awarded 'CoolBrand' status and are invited to join the CoolBrands programme.

Foreword

Angela Cooper
Managing Editor

It gives me great pleasure to introduce this, the sixth volume of CoolBrands.

The brands that feature in this edition come in many different shapes and sizes, from those that have been established and grown over many years to those that are newcomers to the market. As we have found over the course of several years, since the first edition of CoolBrands, defining what is cool is never black and white. It is very subjective and everyone has a different, and often very strong, opinion on what is cool. The consumer now has a vast number of channels available to share their opinions, championing their likes and launching an offensive against their dislikes.

CoolBrands is always a fascinating project to work on as you can almost smell the raw passion of the guardians guiding these brands. Their determination to make their brand succeed in today's tough market conditions is phenomenal.

So how do we decide who is in and who is out? The CoolBrands Council, as well as consumer opinion, is vital to the selection process. At the back of this publication you will find an article written by the Council chairman, Stephen Cheliotis, which details this process and dispels common misconceptions.

I would like to take this opportunity to thank the CoolBrands Council members for their support and involvement in the programme, particularly those who have shared their expertise and thoughts by writing articles especially for this publication. These also appear at the back of the book and investigate the 'cool' arena further.

You will also have noticed our striking cover which was designed by Start Creative, a cross media brand consultancy group, which is now a top 10 independent agency. My thanks also goes to them.

I hope that you enjoy reading this edition of CoolBrands and that it fuels further debate about what's hot and what's not.

CoolBrands Council

2007/08

01 Ralph Ardill
Founder & CEO
The Brand Experience
Consultancy

02 Niku Banaie
Managing Partner
Naked Communications

04 Nicki Bidder
Editor-in-Chief
Dazed & Confused

06 Jodie Dalmeda
Media Consultant

03 Damian Barr
Journalist, Writer,
Playwright & Presenter

05 Paul Croughton
Assistant Travel Editor
The Sunday Times

08 Lee Farrant
Partner
RPM

07 Ekow Eshun
Artistic Director
Institute of
Contemporary Arts

09 Sandra Halliday
Managing Editor
Business Reporting
& Analysis
WGSN.com

10 Andrew Harrison
Associate Editor, The Word
& Editor-in-Chief, Mixmag

12 Dolly Jones
Editor
VOGUE.COM

11 Cozmo Jenks
Milliner

13 Owen Lee
Creative Partner
Farm

14 Gary Robinson
Creative Partner
Farm

15 Ben de Lisi
Fashion Designer

16 **Meritaten Mance**
Co-Founder & Director
Kitchen Communications

17 Simon Mathews
Founding Partner
Rise Communications

18 **Trevor Nelson**
DJ

19 Vaishaly Patel
A-list Facialist

20 Bakul Patki
PR, Production & Project
Development in Arts,
Entertainment & Media

21 **Mary Portas**
Founding Partner &
Creative Director
Yellowdoor

22 Alex Proud
Director
Proud Galleries Ltd

23 Nicolas Roope
Founding Partner
Poke London

24 June Sarpong
Presenter

25 **Tom Savigar**
Partner
The Future Laboratory

26 Dylan Williams
Strategy Director
Mother London

Stephen Cheliotis
Chairman
Superbrands
Councils UK

01 Ralph Ardill
Founder & CEO
The Brand Experience Consultancy

Ralph is recognised as one of the pioneers and leading authorities on experiential branding, design and communication.

In 2005 Ralph set up The Brand Experience Consultancy – a new business venture dedicated to helping brands explore and leverage the commercial, creative and communication possibilities of the emerging experiential economy.

He has, and continues, to consult to some of the world's leading brands, including Guinness, Ford, Ericsson, Coca-Cola, Barclays, Sky, Tate Modern and CBRE on how to best bring their brands to life both inside and outside their organisations and is a regular and accomplished writer, speaker and consultant.

Back in 1995 Ralph wrote one of the first and most provocative books on Experiential Branding – simply entitled 'Experience' – and more recently has written an expert master-class on Experience Design for the UK Design Council.

For the last four years Ralph has also been a special advisor to the Royal Society of Arts and the Parlimentary Design Group.

02 Niku Banaie
Managing Partner
Naked Communications

Niku left Central Saint Martins College in 1999 with awarded work in branding and design, and began his career in the agency world, developing communication ideas for brands such as adidas and Vodafone.

Niku joined his current company, Naked Communications, in 2003, where he is now one of the UK managing partners. As well as expanding the agency Niku still follows his initial calling to generate culturally powerful ideas for household names as well as 'new to the world' brands.

His outside design interests are satisfied through his own furniture range, brothersister, which can be found at the V&A as well as in other stores around Europe.

03 Damian Barr
Journalist, Writer, Playwright & Presenter

Damian, 30, is a journalist, writer, playwright and presenter.

Writing features for The Times, Damian has talked design with Sir Terence Conran, cooked a roast with Hugh Fearnley-Whittingstall and had a manicure with Paris Hilton's mother. He has been diving for scallops and star-gazing in Chile. He has reported on post-Katrina New Orleans and the ever-flooding state of Venice. He also writes for The Independent, The Financial Times, Olive and Country Life. He writes plays for BBC Radio 4, presents a radio series for BBC Scotland and fronts 'Cool In Your Code' – a webTV series for The Times. His first book made the quarterlife crisis a household term. Julie Burchill describes him as "the new ringmaster for the Jerry Springer Generation".

04 Nicki Bidder
Editor-in-Chief
Dazed & Confused

As editor-in-chief of Dazed & Confused, Nicki has been instrumental in the growth of the magazine and the brand at large having worked for the company for seven years. She not only oversees the editorial vision of the title but also its many creative solutions, exhibitions, print products and events that have achieved recognition and influence for the brand beyond the confines of the newsstand. In addition she has been an ongoing consultant for Topshop for six years and continues to work closely with the brand.

05 Paul Croughton
Assistant Travel Editor
The Sunday Times

Paul is a journalist, broadcaster and pop culture commentator who has worked across newspapers, magazines, radio and television – for the BBC, ITV, The Observer, The Times, FHM, Mixmag, Arena, Heat and MTV. He is currently assistant travel editor of The Sunday Times.

06 Jodie Dalmeda
Media Consultant

07 Ekow Eshun
Artistic Director
Institute of
Contemporary Arts

08 Lee Farrant
Partner
RPM

09 Sandra Halliday
Managing Editor
Business Reporting
& Analysis
WGSN.com

10 Andrew Harrison
Associate Editor,
The Word
& Editor-in-Chief,
Mixmag

Jodie is a freelance media consultant for some of the UK's leading marketing and PR agencies. The former head of press for Sony BMG now advises and develops creative media strategies and celebrity endorsements for global brands such as BlackBerry, Virgin Unite, Orange, Moschino, Garrard, MTV, MOBOs and Oxfam.

Jodie has utilised celebrities from both the music and film worlds such as Sean 'P Diddy' Combs, Will Smith, Ashley Walters, Zola 7, Thandie Newton, Richard Ashcroft, Christopher Eccleston, Amir Khan, Gael Garcia Bernal and The Editors to highlight various brand launches and humanitarian campaigns. Jodie was responsible for the media strategy for 'Live 8' South Africa and for creating the global media campaign for the United Nations International Day of Peace.

Jodie specialises in trend forecasting and works with the Prince's Trust as a Specialist Business Advisor. She is also a fellow of the RSA (Royal Society of Arts).

Ekow worked as assistant editor of The Face magazine before being appointed editor-in-chief of Arena magazine, becoming, at 28, the youngest ever editor of a men's magazine.

A high profile writer and broadcaster on art and culture, Ekow makes regular appearances on BBC's Newsnight Review and More4's The Last Word, as well as writing for publications including The Guardian, The Observer and The New Statesman. He has also written and presented several documentaries on TV and radio.

Ekow is a governor of the University of Arts London (2001-present) and a former board member of Tate Members (2003-2005).

His first book, Black Gold of the Sun: Searching for Home in England and Africa, was published by Penguin in June 2005 and was nominated for The Orwell Prize for political writing in 2006.

Lee's early career encompassed sports photography, specialising in Formula One, football and rugby World Cups as well as the Olympics and expedition photography covering the Camel Trophy adventure races.

Lee set up his own photography business in 1990 and formed a design consultancy four years later, in conjunction with RPM. He then joined the experiential marketing specialists as a partner in 1996, where his primary responsibility has been the visual offering of the agency, overseeing design and photography.

Whilst he has worked on projects for a variety of brands, he continues to specialise in working with sports brands to develop consumer strategies and creative implementation platforms. Most recently, Lee has been the driving force behind the globally successful Umbro One Love project. UK and global brands progressed are: Bombay Sapphire, Carlsberg Tetley, Diageo (Bailey's, Smirnoff®, Johnnie Walker), The ECB, The FA, FIFA, Grand Marnier, Grolsch, Land Rover, Martini, Reebok, Umbro, Sky TV and Unilever.

Sandra is managing editor of Business Reporting & Analysis for WGSN.com, the world's leading online fashion forecasting website. In that capacity she identifies and analyses trends for the season ahead, for next year and into the next decade. Prior to this she worked for or edited a variety of business and consumer magazines in the retail, fashion and cosmetics sectors. These included Cosmetic International, Fashion Weekly, Woman, Hair & Beauty, and Tax Free Trader.

Andrew is associate editor of the mature music and entertainment magazine The Word, and editor-in-chief of dance bible Mixmag. Since 2002 he has worked at groundbreaking independent publishers Development Hell Ltd, whose low-overheads and hands-on publishing model has enabled its niche titles to prosper while ungainly larger publishers suffer the vicissitudes of the Web 2.0 revolution.

In the 1990s Andrew edited the award-winning rock monthly Select, which famously identified and named Britpop, and also revolutionised coverage of Glastonbury and other rock festivals to create a model now followed by all rock titles and several broadsheets. He also contributed to The Face, Rolling Stone, Spin, GQ and Arena.

More recently he was editorial director of EMAP's Performance division, where he looked after Q, Mixmag and Smash Hits and launched the girls' gossip weekly Sneak. He has also been music editor at the American men's magazine Details.

11 Cozmo Jenks
Milliner

Recognised as one of Europe's leading milliners, Cozmo has designed hats for some of the world's greatest names: Kylie Minogue, Jamiroquai, Lady Helen Taylor, Viscountess Serena Linley, Jodie Kidd, Jo and Leah Wood, Anya Hindmarch, Pattie Boyd and Brook Shields.

Raised between Hampshire and Dorset, Cozmo's country roots are core to her imaginative designs, drawing inspiration for her vibrant creations from nature and the organic form. Known also for her distinctive personal style, Cozmo combines directional shapes, luxury fabrics and vibrant colours for her whimsical and flamboyant head pieces.

Since starting in millinery 10 years ago, Cozmo has collaborated with many high profile designers including Amanda Wakeley, Tracey Boyd, Buddhistpunk, Steven Fairchild and Maria Grachvogel. Cozmo has also become the first port of call for style ambassadors when dressing for the season's most prestigious weddings, races and events.

Cozmo will soon be launching a slipper collection, 'From Head to Toe', broadening her bespoke luxury offering.

12 Dolly Jones
Editor
VOGUE.COM

Dolly first stepped into the world of Vogue – post-History of Art at Manchester University and wearing Topshop pumps – in 1998 for three weeks work experience that turned into six months as editorial assistant. Next up was the London College of Printing periodical journalism course which commissioned her to interview "someone at the top of their game" – Alexandra Shulman very kindly obliged – and then the 'writer' job at VOGUE.COM came up in January 2000. Seven and a half years later – after breaking news every day, working with the Condé Nast Interactive team to develop and expand the site to its fullest potential including cover archives and VogueTV, and being named editor in 2005 – she is now responsible for a website that boasts 1.3 million unique users per month and was named British Magazine Website of the Year, 2006. Her reward? An upgrade to Manolos.

13&14 Owen Lee & Gary Robinson
Creative Partners
Farm

Gary and Owen started their career globe-trotting through the New York, LA, Sydney and Brisbane offices of the advertising agency Chiat/Day. They settled in Chiat/Day's London office in 1993 and were instrumental in its transformation into St. Luke's in 1995.

They moved from St. Luke's to become a senior creative team at Partners BDDH and after three years they moved to HHCL and Partners. In 2000, they became partners in advertising start-up, Farm.

They have written advertising campaigns for brands including Tango, Pot Noodle, first direct, HSBC, Boots 17, smile.co.uk, Heinz, Virgin Megastores and smart. Their work for Diet Tango and The Co-operative Bank was featured in the Brand New Exhibition at the V&A.

15 Ben de Lisi
Fashion Designer

Ben grew up in New York, where he was taught to sew by his Grandmother, and went on to study sculpture at the Pratt Institute in Brooklyn. In 1982 he moved to London to pursue his dream of becoming a fashion designer and produced his first capsule collection.

Since 1995 Ben has been showing at London Fashion Week, winning the coveted British Glamour Designer of the Year award in 1994 and 1995. He also designs a diffusion line in conjunction with Debenhams – BDL by Ben de Lisi.

In 1998 Ben and his business partner, Debbie Lovejoy, opened their first stand-alone boutique, in Belgravia.

Since 2001 he has been working with Countryside Properties a property developer in North West England, applying his stylish touch to apartments. He is currently working with Abacus, developing a range of branded bathrooms.

Ben has also been involved in TV projects, most recently including his role as a mentor on Project Catwalk.

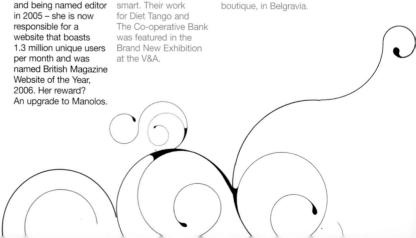

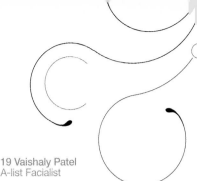

16 Meritaten Mance
Co-Founder & Director
Kitchen Communications

Meritaten started her PR career in the restaurant industry, working with recognised chefs such as Marco Pierre White and The Ivy's Fernando Pierre. Her experiences here and working for Jori White PR, a small lifestyle PR company based in Soho, led to Meritaten becoming joint owner and director of lifestyle PR company, Laundry Communications.

Her achievements were recognised through the successful launch of Roast restaurant in Borough Market and she also enjoyed the enviable title of Prestige Brands Ambassador across Allied Domecq's Champagne and Luxury brands portfolio. Meritaten became co-founder and director of Kitchen Communications in February 2006.

17 Simon Mathews
Founding Partner
Rise Communications

Simon has worked for a number of the advertising groups, most recently running Optimedia International for the Publicis Group before leaving to establish Rise Communications, which is the UK's first value based brand and communication strategy agency specialising in helping brands to profit more from communications. Rise, now four years old, works across a broad portfolio of clients both in the UK and internationally including Cutty Sark Whisky, The COI (energy performance certificates), Richmond Ice Cream and Network Rail. The agency employs a spectrum of skill sets from both the client and agency world, covering disciplines such as broad based communication strategists, data analysts, qualitative researchers, and brand thinking. The common thread is that they are always senior, experienced individuals, who all own part of the business.

Rise has just launched Contented, a digital strategy agency and was recently commended at the Marketing Society awards for its brand launch work for Skinny Cow Ice Cream.

18 Trevor Nelson
DJ

Trevor developed his DJ skills at an early age organising warehouse parties. This led to a slot on the then pirate radio station Kiss FM. In 1990 when Kiss FM became legal, Trevor was offered a daytime show as well as a directorship. He went on to host Radio 1 show, The Rhythm Nation, which was soon followed by a Saturday afternoon show.

Trevor has won DJ of the Year at the MOBO awards twice and has also co-hosted the same awards twice. He continues to DJ across the UK and around the world and host major events and shows across BBC channels, MTV, ITV and Channel 4.

Trevor's passion and drive have enabled him to be one of the champions of R&B music in the UK, and his increasing profile has made him a respected and valued figure in the music industry across the world.

19 Vaishaly Patel
A-list Facialist

Vaishaly is most celebrated for tending the brows of the famous at her stylish Marylebone Village clinic. It is Vaishaly's 'magic' touch, facial massage skills and skin insights that keep many devoted clients returning to her.

Faces are Vaishaly's life-long passion: inspired by an aunt who was a beauty therapist, Vaishaly qualified in beauty therapy, at the London College of Fashion. She went on to work with holistic therapist Bharti Vyas for seven years, evolving her own philosophy about what it takes to achieve great skin while working hands-on. She then set up a practice in Martyn Maxey's Mayfair salon where Vaishaly pioneered the use of microdermabrasion in facials long before it became the beauty 'buzz' it is today.

At the age of 30, Vaishaly opened her own clinic – now a must-visit destination for the likes of Sophie Dahl, Elle Macpherson and Nigella Lawson – where the emphasis is on sublime service and absolute privacy.

20 Bakul Patki
PR, Production & Project Development in Arts, Entertainment & Media

Bakul started working in entertainment whilst studying Art at Central Saint Martins College and then Philosophy at UCL; here she managed bands, worked for various record companies including BMG and Nude Records, and within the music division of one of the original wave of web design studios – (the then) AMXdigital, set up by the prolific designer (Prof) Malcolm Garrett.

After graduating, she worked for a number of other companies, and for the past four years has been a freelance publicist, producer and events co-ordinator; specialising in the arts, entertainment and media.

She often works with independent artists; developing, producing and promoting a variety of projects; particularly in fine art, photography, film and theatre.

Past projects and clients include: The International Herald Tribune's 'Breathless' Art Season, BAFTA nominated and BIFA award-winning independent feature 'Christie Malry's Own Double Entry', West-End theatre production 'Telstar', creative agency yeastCulture, BAFTA, UCTV, Public Artist Martin Firrell, Ecospace Studios & AMP, photographers Tim Foster and Pate Pope, and artist Marc Silver.

21 Mary Portas
Founding Partner & Creative Director
Yellowdoor

Retail marketing guru Mary is quite possibly one of the UK's foremost authorities on retail and brand communication. Previously the creative director of Harvey Nichols, Mary repositioned the brand into the world renowned store and restaurant group it is today.

Mary's foresight and unique knowledge of trends and consumer markets prompted her to launch Yellowdoor in 1997 when she saw a need for integrated and creative brand communication in the retail, fashion, luxury and beauty sectors. Under Mary's guidance, Yellowdoor have created category challenging campaigns for a wide range of brands on the high street including Clarks, Louis Vuitton, Thomas Pink, and French Connection.

Mary writes a weekly column in The Telegraph and has published two books – 'Windows – The art of retail display' and most recently 'How to Shop' with Mary Queen of Shops through BBC books. Mary Queen of Shops, an innovative series on fashion retailing, was launched on BBC2 in May 2007.

22 Alex Proud
Director
Proud Galleries Ltd

Alex established Proud Galleries in 1998, and a host of acclaimed shows such as Destroy – the Sex Pistols, The Rock 'n Roll Years (with the National Portrait Galleries) and Rebel Life – Bob Marley, launched the reputation of Proud Galleries on an international level.

Subsequent shows including Rankin and Bailey Down Under, Rankin's Nudes project, James Dean – the Iconic Images of Phil Stern, Underexposed, True Football, Robbie Williams and Blood & Glitter have cemented the position of Proud Galleries as the most popular private photographic galleries in Europe.

2001 saw the launch of Proud Camden, where groundbreaking shows including Hip Hop Immortals and The Libertines achieved headline coverage and attracted over 2,000 paying visitors every week.

In June 2005, the Camden gallery relocated to Stables Market, Camden Lock, and in 2006, Proud realised a 10-year vision by opening At Proud – a 500-capacity bar and music venue adjacent to the Proud Galleries.

23 Nicolas Roope
Founding Partner
Poke London

From leading creative practitioner and co-founder of Antirom in 1995, though to creative director roles at Oven Digital and Poke, Nicolas has always looked beyond industry rhetoric to the inspiring truths of interactive networked media; this passion has driven his career spanning the last 12 years.

Nicolas jointly set up Poke with veterans from Deep End in 2001 after the dotcom fallout. Since then he has creatively driven numerous high profile accounts and self initiated projects, picking up five Webby Awards and many other world-class accolades along the way.

He is a long standing blogger and frequent contributor to ICON and Design Week and his work and ideas have been widely distributed through the on and off-line worlds.

He has recently been appointed as a member of the Academy of Digital Arts and Sciences and is the UK Webby Ambassador.

Nicolas also founded the Pokia / Hulger project (www.hulger.com), another creative slant on technology, but in this instance, physical.

24 June Sarpong
Presenter

25 Tom Savigar
Partner
The Future
Laboratory

26 Dylan Williams
Strategy Director
Mother London

Stephen Cheliotis
Chairman
Superbrands
Councils UK

June began her TV career at MTV. While there, she presented 'Planet Pop', a segment which was shown on Channel 4's T4. This led, in 1999, to a regular role as front-woman and celebrity interviewer for T4, a role she has held for the last eight years. In this time June has interviewed the likes of Sir Elton John, Kylie Minogue, Black Eyed Peas, Will Smith and Nicole Kidman as well as Tony Blair for T4.

In recent years, June has also presented many other series for E4, the BBC, Channel 5 and most recently 'WAGS Boutique' for ITV.

June has also presented the Smash Hits Poll Winners Party and Party In The Park as well as the MOBO Awards for three consecutive years.

June is an ambassador for the Prince's Trust and also campaigns for the Make Poverty History movement. In 2007 June received an MBE for services to charity.

Tom was previously co-founder and director of Sense Worldwide. Since joining The Future Laboratory in 2005, he has overseen the rapid growth of the company's infrastructure, brand strategy and consumer typology projects, and its work with brands in terms of developing new product and service offers. Clients include Nokia, Lamborghini, Investec Private Bank, Pernod Ricard, Vogue and Gap.

Aside from corporate assignments, Tom enjoys working with the next generation of designers and researchers. He has taught fashion textile students at the University of Brighton how to be keen identifiers of anomalies, the indicators of change, and has formed similar programmes with universities and institutions in Argentina, India, Denmark and Austria.

Tom devotes the majority of his spare time to establishing his fledgling designer menswear label.

Dylan first got lucky on the back of Jamie Oliver in the mid-1990s. Witnessing Jamie's rise to prominence, Dylan figured that by dropping his H's, swearing a bit and hanging out with the homeless, he too could disguise his real origins and stand out in the posh-boy dominated world of advertising. Dylan duly swotted up on Casual culture and, swapping his Horse and Hound for a first edition of Boy's Own, successfully reinvented himself just as everyone fell in love with football at Euro 96. This new positioning quickly paid dividends as he claimed all credit for the advertising on Levi's, Lynx and Audi amongst others. Laughably, he then got voted one of the top two planners in the UK by Campaign magazine. Mindful of the impending collapse of Laddism, Dylan quit as planning director of BBH in 2002 and attempted a rebrand. Inspired by the recent 1980s revival, Dylan changed his name to Leroy and joined Pineapple dance studios.

After a couple of years Dylan grew disenchanted by the confines of Street Jazz and went back to advertising. As strategy director at Mother he now plays a lot of table tennis and continues to wing it. He'll be rumbled eventually as he's not all that really.

Stephen began his career at global brand valuation and strategy consultancy, Brand Finance, where he helped to advise brands on maximising shareholder value through effective brand management. In addition he produced a range of significant reports, including comprehensive studies of global intangible assets. His annual study of City Analysts, which explored the City's need for marketing information, was vital in understanding the importance of marketing metrics in appreciating and forecasting companies' performance.

In 2001 Stephen joined Superbrands UK, becoming UK managing director in 2003 and overseeing two years of significant growth. Given a European role in 2005, his expertise was used across 20 countries. In 2006 he set up his own business providing PR and marketing advice to companies.

Stephen chairs the three independent Superbrands Councils in the UK. He speaks at conferences on branding and is a regular commentator for international media on the subject. He is a frequent guest on CNN, the BBC and Sky amongst others.

INNOVATION
STYLE
DESIRABILITY

Agent Provocateur
Stimulate, enchant and arouse

024

agentprovocateur.com

CoolBrands 2007/08

Joseph Corre and Serena Rees opened the first Agent Provocateur boutique in London's Soho in 1994. What followed was a media frenzy reserved usually for superstars; the response was both exceptional and overwhelming.

Corre and Rees introduced their vision of lingerie to the world, avoiding the British prudery that insisted on categorising anything to do with sex as sleazy or smutty. The aim was to create an availability of high quality designer lingerie with flair to stimulate, enchant and arouse both the wearers and their partners. "A woman wearing a scrumptious pair of knickers promotes in herself a sexy superhero feeling which exudes itself as a confident and positive sexuality."

Agent Provocateur has become a phenomenal success with almost 40 stores worldwide and several more national and international stores in the pipeline. With select store locations, each boutique is an emporium decorated in a boudoir style, featuring seductive and luxurious furnishings to complement the lingerie and indulge the customer. Their carefully handpicked staff wear the famous pink house coat (designed by Vivienne Westwood), which has become a much emulated and iconic glamorous service look. Agent Provocateur also has a thriving mail order catalogue and an award-winning website which receives on average 20,000 plus visitors a day.

The unique way that Corre and Rees established the brand can be seen through the creative communication

of the brand's values, using tools such as its shop windows. From themes such as 'weapons of mass distraction' to subliminal messages of attraction and desire, Agent Provocateur's intimate shopping experience has achieved notoriety through these stunning and stimulating window displays, which have become famous worldwide.

The Agent Provocateur annual media campaign has also become internationally renowned, causing a furore on its launch at the beginning of September each year. Every campaign is sure to offer a ground-breaking creative concept. For example, 'The Four Dreams of Miss X', starring Kate Moss was presented as four short films and photographic stills by Mike Figgis while the 2007/08 campaign, 'The Adventures of Miss A.P', shot by Alice Hawkins, stars an array of strong and beautiful heroines including Maggie Gyllenhaal who takes the lead role in Episode 1. This concept uses several mediums to tell its story, namely striking photographic stills, sexy illustrations and a saucy script.

Agent Provocateur's cinema advertising, catalogues and events, books and all other sensual lifestyle products have all attracted massive national and international media coverage, firmly securing Agent Provocateur as one of the only truly credible lingerie brands on the fashion map, spawning a subsequent explosion of lingerie into the fashion world. The unique brand has become a household name and has recently been awarded an MBE from the Queen for its services to the British fashion industry.

Corre and Rees have always understood the important marriage between scent and seduction and hence, in 2000 Agent Provocateur launched its first fragrance, the Signature Eau de Parfum. Presented in an egg-shaped porcelain bottle, the perfume has won the most

prestigious of beauty awards, a Fifi award for best fragrance, and has since become a modern classic. In 2007 Agent Provocateur did it again with their second female perfume, Maîtresse, winning Fifi's Best Women's Fragrance of 2006 award.

At the heart of Agent Provocateur is a profound belief in the intimacy of the experience that it offers – described by its co-founders as "the difference between a mass experience, dictated by market forces and meaningless advertising, and an intensely private, wholly personal experience". This, with the garment that he or she selects, is realised by the company through quality, service and an absolute refusal to adhere to fluctuating trends. As Agent Provocateur enters its 14th year, it remains committed to investment in creativity led by pure instinct of that which is beautiful, and of course erotic.

Remember, there is an Agent Provocateur in everyone just waiting to be unleashed.

Alexander McQueen
Tradition doesn't always mean convention

alexandermcqueen.com

CoolBrands 2007/08

Inspiring, spectacular, romantic: just some of the words used over the years to describe Alexander McQueen's visionary designs.

At the age of 16, McQueen turned his back on conventional education in favour of an apprenticeship at Savile Row tailors Anderson and Shepherd – before moving on to neighbouring outfitters Gieves & Hawkes. While both establishments were widely respected for technical skill in garment construction it was at theatrical costumiers, Angels and Bermans, that McQueen really mastered the art of pattern cutting. From the melodramatic structures of 16th century styling to the brutally sharp tailoring that was to become part of his signature style, the designer honed his talents through six different disciplines.

McQueen went on to prove his credentials, working with London-based designer Koji Tatsuno. Still only 21 years-old, McQueen moved to Milan as design assistant to couturier Romeo Gigili. Returning to London a year later, he completed a Masters degree in fashion design at the prestigious Central Saint Martins. McQueen's degree show caused a media sensation – fashion journalist Isabella Blow (who became a great supporter and source of inspiration) bought the entire collection.

McQueen's eponymous label, that combined lyrical romanticism with aggressive tailoring, courted controversy from the start. The catwalk shows were pure theatre, often inspired by cult celluloid classics, but even high drama couldn't disguise the craftsmanship, cut and impeccable detail of each design.

This is reflected in McQueen being named 'British Designer of the Year' four times, in 1996, 1997, 2001 and again in 2003.

In 2003, McQueen was also awarded International Designer of the Year by The Council of Fashion Designers of America and was honoured in the same month with a CBE for his services to the British fashion industry.

At the tender age of 27, and with only eight full collections behind him, McQueen was appointed designer-in-chief at Givenchy before eventually joining forces with the Gucci Group in 2000.

In partnership with Gucci, McQueen finally achieved what he had been craving: a greater creative license. With the Italian fashion house's financial support and active encouragement of his creative talents, the label has developed into an internationally recognised brand.

The McQueen brand is primarily promoted through its shows – which remain the key promotional tool. Every show is treated as a presentation of the concept behind each collection; the idea being to present an artistic and emotional experience to the audience that will invariably provoke thought and reaction. For McQueen what matters most is that there is a reaction – it doesn't always have to be 'good', just as long as the audience is left with a lasting image. If this occurs then he believes his (and the brand) objective has been met.

The shows differentiate the brand through embodying a strong non-comprising aesthetic and vision. Each is personal to McQueen and as a result has an artistic integrity that contributes to the quintessential 'coolness' of the brand. The message extends way beyond fashion – fashion is merely the vehicle.

Today the brand has flagship stores in New York, Milan and London; a fragrance, 'Kingdom'; a menswear collection; and eyewear.

Over the years, Alexander McQueen has presented an ongoing fairytale steeped in drama and mystery that has earned him the highest esteem amongst the fashion elite. His Spring/Summer 2007 collection offered up a typically theatrical turn of the century dark romance combined with the technical skills of tomorrow. Inspired in equal parts by fantasy and reality, past and present, McQueen continues to stand out in an increasingly homogenous world thanks to the originality of his striking designs.

Anna Sui
Fantasy
rocks! Live
your dream.

028

Anna Sui is a classic American success story: from the Detroit suburbs to downtown New York, a childhood dream and love of fashion fostering a trendsetting brand with a penchant for the unconventional.

The creative force behind the eponymous brand – Anna Sui – uses her eclectic style to steer its direction. Brought up in Dearborn, Michigan, Anna's predilections were apparent from an early stage as she wiled away hours dressing up neighbours' toy soldiers and creating her 'Genius Files' – clippings from fashion magazines and papers that were (and still are) used for inspiration.

Anna's overriding passion to become a designer never waivered; a move to New York at aged 17 – to Parson's School of Design – secured her future in fashion. It was here that she met and did styling for photographer, Steven Meisel.

She launched her own collection in 1981 out of her apartment. The brand continued to grow throughout the next decade, putting on its first catwalk show in 1991, where she paid supermodels, Linda Evangelista and Naomi Campbell, in clothes – a non-conformist approach that continues to guide its ethos today.

The following year Anna Sui opened her first flagship store in New York's trendy Soho district. The boutique's vibrant mix of purple walls, black Victoriana and papier-mâché dolly-heads created a romantic, rock 'n' roll ambience – closely reflecting its founder's personal style – that was to become the mainstay model

for all subsequent shops. Today Anna Sui has 32 boutiques in five countries and its collection is sold in 300 stores, ranging across 30 countries.

During the late 1990s Anna Sui launched its accessories, cosmetics and fragrance collection in the Far East. The brand's attention to detail – from iconic packaging to bottle design – quickly established a cult fan-base that elevated the range to collector status. Each scent bottle is unique with the Dolly Girl collection showcasing a different 'Dolly Head' shaped bottle to accompany every new fragrance.

In 1997, Anna Sui joined forces with Wella AG of Germany (now a division of P&G Prestige Products) to develop a signature fragrance. In a trilateral arrangement P&G now shares the Anna Sui beauty business with Japanese cosmetics maker, Albion.

Anna Sui's fragrances aim to offer a gateway to an 'other-wordly' feminine retreat where reality merges with fantasy. Each has a definitive personality made up of fragments of Anna's own personality. For example, Sui Dreams represents fantasy with attitude, the essence of Anna's philosophy: 'Live your dream! If you have a vision … follow it, you alone can make anything happen.'

By using magical motifs on products such as the butterfly, roses and fairies, the brand conjurs up an almost ethereal air, creating an enchanted boudoiresque world brimming with fantasy and irony; a romantic antidote to the corporate hard-edged styling favoured by many modern designers.

This dreamlike vision extends to brand advertising, seen for example in the Secret Wish Magic Romance campaign where celebrity model, Anne Watanabe – surrounded by hearts, butterflies and

twinkling stars – represents a sensual, Secret Wish Magic Romance siren.

Over the years Anna has been honoured with a host of awards for her ongoing contribution to fashion and her fragrances also continue to accumulate accolades. Secret Wish was voted 'Best Launch' in a 2006 online vote and the following year won Best Choice Fragrance in the Vogue Beauty Awards.

Anna Sui is a multi-faceted personality: unconventional, provocative and fun. Inspiration is sourced from a variety of directions, from the romantic frills of rococo clothes to hippie chic, always with a rock 'n' roll edge – a convergence of influences and ideas from the past, present and future that continue to define the brand.

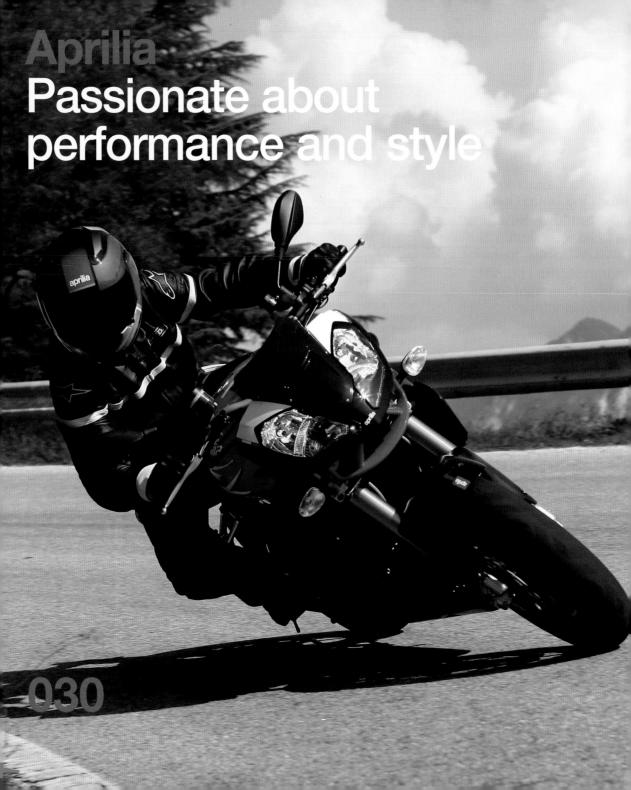

Aprilia
Passionate about performance and style

030

aprilia.com

CoolBrands 2007/08

Aprilia's origins date back to the end of World War II when Cavalier Alberto Beggio founded a factory in Noale, a province of Venice, to manufacture bicycles.

His son, Ivano, joined the business in 1968 and with the help of a dozen Aprilia employees, built the first Aprilia motorbike: a gold and blue 50cc model. It was clear from this point forward where the direction of the brand lay.

The initial model (along with Aprilia's first moped designs that followed) was well received but it wasn't until 1970, and the launch of the Scarabeo cross bike, that the brand really got noticed. The Scarabeo quickly became the 'must-have' item for those with their sights set on competing in national competitions. Engine sizes ranged from 50 to 125cc and the models included aesthetic features such as metallic gold paintwork, which was to become a characteristic of all Aprilia products. The iconic Scarabeo cross bike spawned the RC125 and heralded the start of a strong affinity between sports and standard production, now a hallmark of the Noale factory.

During the late 1970s the factory expanded activities beyond Italy's border with the American market proving particularly significant. The decade ended on a high: from 1969 to 1979 annual production of mopeds went from 150 to 12,000 units, with motorbike production growing to more than 2,000 units per year.

Aprilia's commercial success was consolidated during the 1980s when it became the market leader in motorbikes

for the younger generation, with models such as ST, ETX and AF1. During this period its range was expanded to include models from 50 to 600cc and the brand took on new challenges in the form of world rallies and the Grand Prix Championship. The decade of sustained growth that followed saw Aprilia become Europe's second largest motorcycle manufacturer, its reputation for cutting-edge design corroborated by the launch of the first scooter to make major use of plastics in its construction. Further innovation followed in 1995, when it joined forces with renowned designer, Philippe Starck. The result: the Moto 6.5, a model that has since acquired a cult following.

Aprilia is an unconventional brand, not only in its pioneering design and use of technology but also in its structure and organisation; strategic planning, design and marketing still being concentrated in its historical home of Noale where the company's Logistics Centre is also based. This occupies an area of nearly 70,000 sq m – 31,000 sq m indoors. In 2005 Aprilia completed its integration into Europe's biggest manufacturer of powered two wheelers, the Piaggio Group, and became fully part of the company.

Now a leading name on the world's racing circuits, Aprilia has established itself as one of the most prestigious and successful marques over its relatively short history. Since 1985, when it first entered the World Speed Championships, the company has won 32 world titles. It has also accrued prestigious awards that include Masterbike 2006, for the RSV1000R which has proved itself against the very best that the Japanese and rest of the world have to offer – still winning awards nearly 10 years after its introduction.

While Aprilia's short term objective is to break into the strategic markets of China and India – the two countries that now account for the sale of most of the world's vehicle production – its primary focus remains unchanged: to produce specialist motorcycles and sophisticated scooters that combine class, innovation and the very best in Italian engine technology.

Asahi

Japanese for 'rising sun'.
Shine.

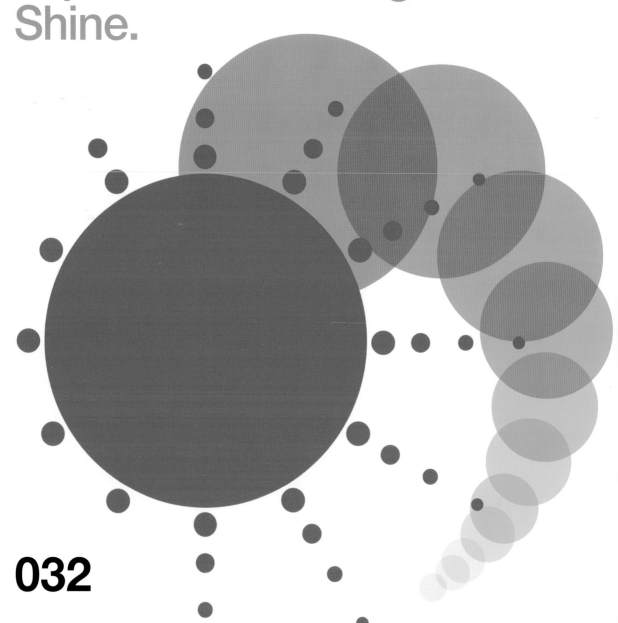

asahibeer.co.uk

Asahi is Japanese for 'rising sun' a symbol of spirit, hope, and inspiration. The brand has a proud history dating back 117 years and has a reputation for creating products strongly influenced by its Japanese heritage that are modern, stylish and innovative.

Asahi launched its core product, Asahi Super Dry, in Japan in 1987 and the rest of the world soon after. Now sold in more than 25 countries, Asahi Super Dry's exacting standards, distinct crisp flavour and urban appeal have helped boost its global sales year-on-year. Since its UK launch in 1998, Asahi Super Dry has become a top-selling imported premium beer in hotspots and bars nationwide, and in 2006 was introduced – following a series of successful test trials – in draught form. Having exceeded expectations (in terms of market demand and sales) Asahi draught is now served in leading gastropubs, clubs and bars throughout the UK along with its bottled counterpart.

Asahi's core belief that 'quality is more important than quantity' is reinforced through its tailored marketing and sales approach. Venues that ooze aspirational style and have an eye for modern design are chosen to showcase the brand. For example, Asahi Super Dry is the only draught offering at the newly opened Park Plaza County Hall on London's South Bank. In addition, many leading celebrity venues such as Amica, Alphabet, China White, Lab, Raffles and Valmont offer the premium bottled product.

As key sponsor for the 2007 Brighton Fringe Festival, Asahi Super Dry was the top seller at UdderBelly – a flamboyant purple cow shaped venue that played host to the latest 'must-see' acts on the comedy and music circuits. Asahi's high profile presence at major alternative arts events – such as exhibitions at the White Cube Gallery (including Damien Hirst's) – and its sponsorship of Sunshine, the 2007 movie from maverick British film director Danny Boyle, reinforce the brand direction. Its aim: to appeal to the discerning consumer who is attracted by the brand's effortless 'in the know' status. It is this consistent marketing approach that convinces the consumer of the brand's credibility.

Asahi's advertising reinforces the positive symbolism of the 'rising sun' with the brand idea 'Shine'. The 2007 activity took advantage of the longest day of the year by asking consumers to celebrate the many hours of sunlight with Asahi and shine.

The campaign, created by advertising agency Hooper Galton, features graphic

designs by students from renowned colleges such as Central Saint Martins College of Art and Design and the London College of Communication. The students were commissioned to create individual interpretations of the rising sun. The multi-media campaign – officially marked by an 'up-and-coming' music event at the Park Plaza Riverbank – has a visible market presence via a range of media; digital escalator panels, trade press, aspirational lifestyle magazines such as ID and GQ, distinct online display advertising and a totally re-worked interactive website.

Asahi's ongoing marketing success owes much to the integrated approach it takes to all of its communications. A distinct brand energy flows through every line of the marketing mix so the brand's position at the forefront of imported premium beers looks set to continuously 'shine'.

Tomorrow is the longest day. Prepare to shine.

Asahi is Japanese for 'rising sun'. A symbol of spirit, hope and inspiration. **Shine**

New 'rising sun' by Noriko Takamori   www.asahibeer.co.uk

Aston Martin
Power, beauty and soul

A strong racing heritage, coupled with exceptional craftsmanship and quality, has made Aston Martin what it is today: a globally recognised name with a reputation for understated elegance and style.

In 1914, engineers and racing drivers, Lionel Martin and Robert Bamford, joined forces to create racing cars. They named their company after the Aston Clinton Hill Climb Course in Buckinghamshire, where Martin had triumphed with lightweight specials. After early racing success the focus switched to road cars, with the pioneering Atom saloon making its debut during World War II. Post-war, under the charismatic ownership of David Brown, Aston Martin became famous for its DB series of saloons. The DBR1 sports model enjoyed considerable track success and paved the way for a succession of high performing models such as the V8, Virage, DB7 and Vanquish. The brand's motorsport heritage has been revitalised in recent years through new racing-specific models and high profile victories at celebrated courses such as Le Mans.

As the leading British manufacturer of high performance sporting GTs, Aston Martin's current line-up – the V8 Vantage, V8 Vantage Roadster, DB9 and DB9 Volante – has recently been joined by a fifth product, the new flagship DBS. Each model is produced at its award-winning factory in Gaydon, Warwickshire by a skilled workforce that combines traditional hand-finishing with high-tech manufacturing and modern materials.

Since 1964 – when Sean Connery first drove a DB5 in the film Goldfinger –

Aston Martin has been indelibly linked to the James Bond series. This high-profile cinematic partnership continued in 2006 with the Aston Martin DBS featuring in the latest Bond outing, Casino Royale, starring the new 007, Daniel Craig.

Aston Martin's distinctive winged logo (believed to denote speed) first appeared in 1927, and has evolved, over time, to maintain a contemporary look. Today, each car has a discreet metal badge on the bonnet and boot while inside, the logo plays a key role in conveying the brand values; in the DB9, for example, the logo is sand-etched onto the crystal starter button, which illuminates red when the ignition is on, before changing to blue. All showrooms also display a version of the logo, rendered in stainless steel and illuminated by LED lights.

The brand's global dealership programme features an award-winning series of new-build pavilions at prime locations in South Africa, Australia and Japan, the US, Hong Kong, France, Italy and Spain. The pavilion-style showrooms are marked (like the brand's products) by a strong emphasis on design and attention to detail – reflecting Aston Martin's tradition of craftsmanship and bespoke service; the effect more reminiscent of a boutique hotel than a conventional car showroom.

In a recent poll, the readers of professional website 'Car Design News' voted the Aston Martin V8 Vantage as

their favourite current production car design. The Vantage V8 and DB9 have also been recipients of the prestigious 'Car of the Year' award from Robb Report, Auto Motor und Sport, Autocar and Top Gear magazine.

In June 2007 Aston Martin began a new chapter in its history when it was sold to a consortium led by David Richards, John Sinders, Investment Dar and Adeem Investment – ending almost 20 years as part of Ford Motor Company. The partnership, overseen by Dr Ulrich Bez (CEO of Aston Martin since July 2000), offers opportunities for continued new product development and enhancement that includes the launch in 2009 of the Aston Martin Rapide.

Throughout its history, Aston Martin has successfully embraced change without compromising its worldwide reputation; each design combining form, function and material to produce aesthetic beauty, sporting prowess and luxury.

Aveda
Natural
beauty

036

Aveda – the art and science of pure flower and plant essences – develops, manufactures and markets an extensive collection of plant-based hair care, skin care, makeup, Pure-Fume™ and lifestyle products.

Aveda can be found in more than 8,000 salons, spas and Experience Centers around the world as well as being available in many salons and department stores in the UK. Colours in Aveda's makeup for face, lips and eyes reflect the vibrancy of nature's palette. Its skincare formulas are plant-packed to infuse skin with radiance and haircare products use nature's power to defy damage.

Entrepreneur, environmentalist and well-being guru Horst Rechelbacher, founded the brand in 1978. His goal was to provide beauty industry professionals with high performance, botanically based products. To achieve this, he pursued the study of Ayurveda, its origins in Eastern science and philosophy and its relationship to the essences and elements found in nature.

From his home in Minneapolis, Horst developed Aveda using plant extracts from around the globe, grown without petrochemial fertilizers, insecticides or herbicides. Aveda's head office is still in Minneapolis, set in 65 acres surrounded by wetlands, with most rooms receiving direct sunlight via picture windows and skylights.

Aveda's philosophy is to offer positive choices for living life in balance – with ones self, each other and the Earth.

Its ingredients are sustainably sourced – for the least impact on the planet and the indigenous cultures Aveda works in partnership with.

Aveda practices what it preaches when it comes to environmental responsibility and is constantly striving to do more. Its responsibility starts with the ingredients it sources. As of June 2006, 80 per cent of the tonnage of essential oils purchased by Aveda for use in manufacturing its products were certified organic.

It is a member of the Coalition for Environmentally Responsible Economies (CERES), a national network of investment funds, environmental organisations and other public interest groups working to advance environmental stewardship on the part of businesses.

Aveda is also an industry leader in environmentally responsible packaging. In 2005, it was the first to use a cap containing 25 per cent post-consumer recycled (PCR) material for some shampoos and conditioners. This follows other packaging firsts for the company: Aveda uses 80-100 per cent PCR HDPE in its bottles and jars, which, calculations show, reduces the use of virgin high density polyethylene by 300 tons annually.

Aveda partners with traditional communities in an effort to bring high-quality ingredients, better traceability in its supply chain and a more positive effect for those who need it most. Among Aveda's partners are the Mardu peoples of Western Australia, the Yawanawa people of the Western Amazon, and babassu nut gatherers in North-eastern Brazil.

Further to this, its research and developments into plant-derived ingredients is ongoing, with both new ingredients and the replacement of existing ones with greener alternatives being investigated, to maintain the high standards that Aveda was founded on.

Beck's
Four Steps
to Purity

038

Made in strict accordance with the German purity law 'Reinheitsgebot', Beck's has been brewed in Bremen, Germany to the same recipe since 1873. Today, some 600 people produce seven million bottles each day – just enough to keep up with global demand.

Since its launch in the UK in 1984, Beck's has established itself as the leading imported lager in the UK market with latest figures illustrating a resurgence in the brand's popularity, growing by 25 per cent across total trade, year-on-year (Source: Nielsen GB MAT March 2007). The brand's focus on purity lies at the heart of its success; the 'Reinheitsgebot' guarantees that only four all-natural ingredients – barley-malt, hops, yeast and water – are permitted in the brewing process. This strict regulation (dating back to 1516) produces the crisp, fresh taste Beck's is renowned for internationally. An unwavering dedication to quality and purity is shared by Beck's Vier, an imported four per cent ABV lager brewed to the same exacting standards as Beck's.

Several key inventions have furthered Beck's pioneering quest to brew the 'perfect' beer. Examples include the Linde Cooling Machine, which helped to revolutionise the brewing process; before its invention, beer could only be produced in March each year, high summer temperatures detrimentally affecting quality and taste.

Beck's progressive and innovative spirit aims to appeal to consumers who value authenticity. Brand advertising has

always been underpinned by its brewing credentials and product quality; attributes reflected in its 'Four Steps' television advertising campaign. The symbolism of the number four – a quartet of dancing characters repeatedly dancing the same four steps – celebrates the precision with which Beck's is brewed.

In 2007 this campaign has been bolstered by a bold digital 'out of home' strategy to reflect the values and lifestyle of modern, urban consumers; appearing on transvision screens across the UK's busiest train stations, digital escalator panels on the London Underground and interactive online advertising.

Staying true to a modern contemporary attitude that values style and culture, Beck's has been working with art's leading lights for over 20 years. Artists such as Damian Hirst, Tracey Emin, and the Chapman Brothers to name but a few have worked with Beck's on a very unusual canvas – designing limited edition bottle labels.

Up until 1999, Beck's association with contemporary art primarily took the form of a series of ambitious commissions such as Rachel Whiteread's plaster cast of the interior of an East London terrace house, as well as the sponsorship of a selection of national exhibition openings. In 1999 Becks teamed up with the Institute of Contemporary Arts (ICA) to cement its role in the UK art scene and Beck's Futures, a competition platform to launch up and coming UK artists, was born.

In 2007 the brand's involvement in contemporary culture took a leap forward with Beck's Fusions. At four landmark events headline performances dynamically fused together leading figures in the art and music worlds. 9,000 competition winners donned 3D glasses at Trafalgar Square to witness an immersive performance from Calvin Harris and Novak 3D Disco, followed by an awe inspiring display from the The Chemical Brothers and United Visual Artists.

Beck's Fusions also took place at iconic locations in Dublin, Manchester and Glasgow. Every event drew on both national and regional art talent to create an electrifying audio-visual experience exhibited in a vast orbital touring gallery, which was free to all in the run up to the headline shows. Beck's Fusions was strikingly brought to life by a series of intriguing hybrid characters built up of items from tubes of paint to jack leads. Appearing animated online, across key press titles and outdoor including colossal building projections, the characters illustrated the powerful fusion of art and music.

Berghaus
Scaling the heights of outdoor performance wear

berghaus.com

CoolBrands 2007/08

By working with some of the world's leading outdoor activists – from mountaineers and walkers through to mountain bikers and trail runners – Berghaus has pushed the boundaries of what is possible with outdoor performance wear.

In 1966, the LD Mountain Centre opened in Newcastle upon Tyne. This was the first specialist outdoor shop in the area in what was a fledgling and niche market in the UK. The shop's owners also distributed outdoor gear from Europe around the UK and needed a name for that part of their business. As much of the best kit at that time came from Germany or Austria, they rightly decided that a bit of instant credibility could be gained for their distribution arm by roughly translating the name of their shop into German. And so Berghaus was born.

It wasn't long before the shop's owners started to make their own products to sell and they branded this new kit with the Berghaus name. The brand quickly built up a reputation for itself in the UK and in 1974, the company launched a revolutionary product that helped to confirm its status as an innovator – Cyclops, the world's first internal framed load carrying rucksack. Today, whether you're climbing the toughest peak, scaling the highest rock face, backpacking on a long distance trail or skiing off piste, Berghaus has a range of clothing, footwear, rucksacks and accessories that will keep you warm, dry and comfortable to get the most out of your outdoor experience.

Over the years, Berghaus has further enhanced its reputation for being at the forefront of outdoor performance technology by continuing to develop new, cutting-edge products. Each season the experienced product team utilises not only their own first-hand knowledge, but also that of renowned outdoor athletes and extreme sportspeople such as Sir Chris Bonington and Leo Houlding.

In 2007 Berghaus launched the Ator collection – high performance multi-activity outdoor products with a contemporary design and feel – timing this to coincide with the opening of the first Berghaus flagship store in Gateshead's MetroCentre. A further new line was also developed ready for 2008 – 365Life incorporates organic cottons, recycled fabrics, vegetable tanning and other natural materials, demonstrating the brand's evolution and commitment to reducing the environmental impact of its products. 2007 also saw Berghaus venture into the Japanese market for the first time and marked the beginning of a

collaboration with directional fashion design label Griffin. Both brand extensions were aimed at raising the brand profile and broadening its appeal.

The Berghaus brand symbolises a true spirit of adventure that is evident within its people and products and is internationally renowned for quality and high performance. For many years the Berghaus brand has been recognised beyond the outdoor industry; broadcasters, presenters, actors, pop stars, celebrities and even royalty all having been caught on camera wearing the brand's products. Berghaus is not, by definition, a fashion brand but it has always been fashionable, generating a 'must have' reputation. This was epitomised in 2006, when the company launched its first ever cinema campaign, featuring sponsored climber Leo Houlding. The commercial was shown nationwide before the James Bond movie Casino Royale, exposing the brand to its widest ever audience.

There is little point in having a product if there's no-one around to use it; it's the people who make Berghaus what it is and have built it into the leader that it is today. As the industry focus is increasingly placed upon innovation and technology, Berghaus clothing, footwear and equipment continues to rise to the challenge, utilising its strong heritage to prepare with confidence for the future mountains it has to climb.

WHAT HIS MOTHER WOULD MAKE HIM WEAR
IF SHE KNEW WHAT HE WAS DOING

berghaus
TRUST IS EARNED

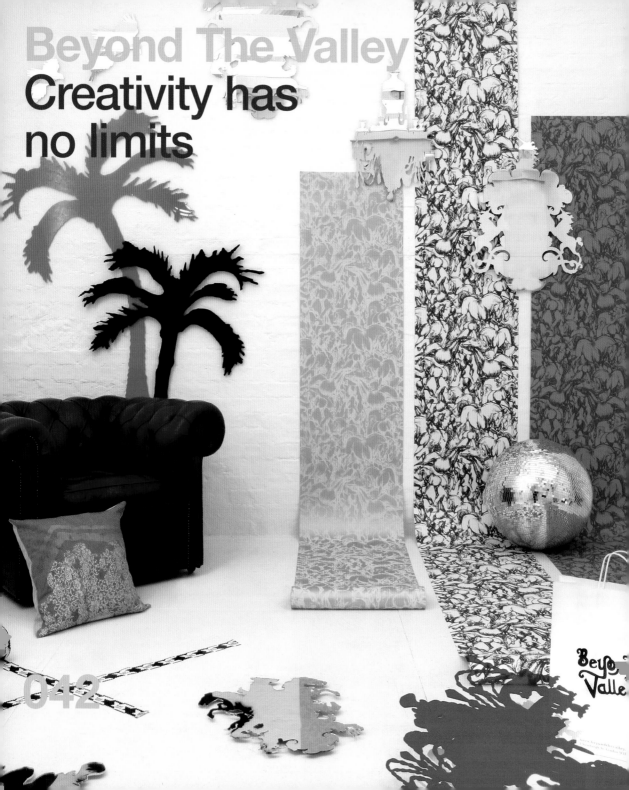

Beyond The Valley
Creativity has no limits

042

In 2003, in response to the lack of advice and commercial opportunities available for new designers, three Central Saint Martins graduates decided to launch their own spring-board for Creatives. The result was Beyond The Valley.

The initial concept – to promote and develop the work of emerging designers and artists – remains, with brand co-founders Jo Jackson, Kate Harwood, and Kristjana Williams still committed to its fundamental principle. But in the four years since inception, the brand has expanded beyond its original remit and is now on its way to becoming an international creative tour-de-force.

After initially testing the waters in temporary outlets in London's Covent Garden, a key stage in the brand's development came with the opening of the brand's first permanent shop in Newburgh Street. Located in the heart of Soho, the concept store – including studio and gallery space – offers the ideal platform for Beyond The Valley's cutting-edge style; stocking both an exclusive range of Beyond The Valley fashion and design products as well as up-and-coming labels such as Yuko Yoshitake, Hulger and the Chatwin Bros.

The Newburgh Street store is one of the brand's unique selling points, offering the opportunity for showcasing own-brand innovations and designs to a selective audience before producing them on a larger scale for selected boutiques, design stores and galleries, as well as for a host of international clients. The store

is the first key stage in Beyond The Valley's quest to balance art with accessibility and commercial viability.

Current Beyond The Valley in-store products include limited edition fashion collections, laser-cut mirrors and exclusive hand-printed wallpaper. Its Autumn/Winter 2007/08 men and women's wear range is playfully elegant with satin trimmed jackets and velvet kimono tops, alongside the brand's signature graphic silk-screened t-shirts. By forging strong links with new designers graduating from the leading arts universities (in particular University of the Arts London), Beyond The Valley ensures that it stays ahead of current trends, both in its London store and internationally, via its own-brand range.

One distinctive brand innovation is the idea of creating guerrilla stores, the first one arriving in Helsinki in 2005. In collaboration with its mother sponsor Contra – a Finnish international creative agency – Beyond The Valley set up the temporary shop in the heart of Helsinki's retail shopping district, remaining in situ for two months. This pivotal point provided a catalyst for the brand's international expansion. A similar concept is currently being planned for Shanghai with expansion plans focused on setting up identical 'temporary' outlets globally as an annual event.

As illustrated by its guerrilla stores, Beyond The Valley tends to bypass the more conventional forms of marketing in favour of word-of-mouth and more subversive forms of brand promotion. Unusual events, exhibitions and party evenings, regularly hosted at various locations in and around the capital, attract an eclectic range of people. These 'out-of-hour' events have contributed to increasing brand awareness and helped to establish a growing consumer base that provides

the basis for the next planned phase of the brand's international expansion.

As a multi-faceted enterprise, Beyond The Valley is not limited by the restrictions of the retail industry. Already identified by the press as 'one to watch', future plans include expanding the range and availability of its own products in leading retail outlets. Commercial growth, however, doesn't necessarily mean treading the corporate path. The essence of Beyond The Valley has always been, and remains, decidedly hands-on.

Store Gallery

Modern fashion with a vintage past

It was in 1964, at the height of the swinging sixties, that ex-fashion illustrator Barbara Hulaniki unleashed the BIBA experience on London's hip young things. The trendsetting label made an immediate impact thanks to its distinctive designs, affordability and non-conformist approach.

BIBA was initially launched as a modest mail order company but its literal overnight success (a pink gingham design advertised in a national newspaper accruing over 4,000 orders by the following morning) soon led to the opening of its first store, a small fashion boutique in Abingdon Street, West London.

In the early 1970s BIBA appropriated a seven storey building in High Street Kensington, becoming the first new department store to open in London since World War II. The expansion saw the label diversify beyond clothing into the likes of food and home furnishings. BIBA was selling a lifestyle and by 1975 had been instrumental in transforming London into one of the world's most fashionable cities. Amongst the legions of fans that flocked to its Kensington flagship store were Brigitte Bardot, Twiggy, Yoko Ono and Mick and Bianca Jagger; but it wasn't purely a haunt for the rich and famous, its cutting-edge couture and affordability attracting BIBA devotees from all walks of life, from students and rock stars to shop girls and housewives.

BIBA also broke new ground by becoming the first major high street name to break retail conventions of the time, going out of its way to experiment with marketing strategies. Its innovative interior was deliberately laid out to enhance the clothes, draping them over coat stands rather than hanging them up. Nothing was ever displayed in BIBA store windows; customers were instead seduced inside by tantalising glimpses of the sumptuous interiors within. It wasn't just through its designs that BIBA was ahead of its time, it was also the first retail outlet to let customers test makeup before buying it, starting the now widespread trend for 'try before you buy'.

BIBA's striking logo, a black and gold art deco design by Antony Little, was key to its success. Not only did it mirror the Art Nouveau feel of the Abingdon Street store's interior – which, with blacked out windows, had no natural light – it also set a standard in branding; BIBA was the first high street label to create its own look. The logo was used on all of its products, creating an instantly recognisable identity whether it was on clothes, food or wallpaper.

The brand's phenomenal success, however, could not be sustained; in 1975 BIBA closed and – as Alwyn Turner comments in his book, The BIBA Experience – fulfilled the old rock 'n' roll promise to "Live fast, die young and leave a beautiful corpse". But the story didn't end there; in 2006 BIBA rose like a phoenix, it's new collection unveiled to critical acclaim at London Fashion Week.

The revamped BIBA offers more than homage to its past legacy, combining modern day aesthetics with the boldness of spirit and innovative design that characterised the brand during its heyday. Tasking some of today's most dynamic UK designers, such as Bella Freud, with producing its new collections

the new look BIBA is a very British affair, combining a fresh and modern design ethos with the rock 'n' roll renegade spirit of the label's memorable past. Its Summer 2007 collection marries the spirit of a new London with eclectic prints in yellow and magenta, while polka dot shoes and bags complement vintage-look psychedelic jewellery.

BIBA was the first label to make fashion accessible and shopping a leisure activity. Today, BIBA is sold throughout the world in 23 countries through luxury retailers like Harrods, Bergdorf Goodman and Fred Segal with flagship stores due to open in 2008 in London, Los Angeles and Las Vegas. London's most legendary fashion label takes on the world once again...

Brabantia
Functional
Timeless
Desirable

046

brabantia.com

CoolBrands 2007/08

Brabantia's ambition is simple: to develop timeless and functional household products that retain their beauty and performance for up to 20 years; it's what drives the company.

It all began in 1919 with 15 people and a small factory in the Dutch Province of Noord-Brabant, from which the company took its name – a traditional, family owned business, run by engineers and craftsmen.

Right from the start, professional workmanship has been the driving force behind Brabantia's success, making products designed to provide years of problem-free use. Designed for the present, but with an eye to the future, they stand out due to their high-quality, functional design, durability and user-friendly features.

The Brabantia of today is modern and dynamic, but still remains a family owned company, and has grown to become one of the leading suppliers of high quality household products worldwide.

The brand is expanding, with production facilities in the Netherlands, Belgium, the UK and China, and will be moving into Latvia in the near future. Sales are overseen by the company's own sales organisations in almost all EU-countries, Hong Kong and the US as well as via a worldwide network of partners that work together with more than 900 'Brabantians' to provide service and product guarantees.

Brabantia operates in several product areas, namely waste collection, laundry care, food storage, food preparation, post boxes (for the home) and bathroom

items. As one of the leading brands in the houseware industry, product innovation plays a very important role in the Brabantia strategy, maintaining a flow of new products to the market.

Recent examples of this pioneering spirit include the award-winning Touch Bin® range which features a 'Soft-Touch' opening and closing system. In addition to this, Brabantia has developed a Sensor Bin, eliminating the need to touch the bin at all with its sensor activated opening and closing mechanism.

In laundry, the WallFix dryer launched in 2007. Designed to fold away when not in use, this wall mounted dryer offers 25 meters of drying space when open. Its launch was supported by a TV commercial demonstrating the space-saving properties of the product.

Brabantia's products have been recognised for their design excellence. In 2006 its innovative SmartLift rotary dryer was awarded an iF product design award by International Forum Design, widely regarded as one of the most prestigious international product design accolades, attracting over 1,800 entries from 30 different countries each year.

Over the years advertising has played an important role in Brabantia's marketing communication. Work includes international media campaigns as well as national and local marketing activities – always with the same 'solid' message.

The current campaign reflects the brand's commitment to durability, an area in which Brabantia has built a reputation. A valuable asset to the brand, this standing is reinforced by all Brabantia products carrying long term guarantees.

Brabantia has been awarded ISO 14001 certification for environmental care and places great importance on environmental issues. In addition to this, it supports and subscribes to the statements of the UN on child labour and does not accept forced labour.

Brabantia's approach to business is summed up by the brand as 'Solid Company'.

Buddhistpunk
Rock 'n' roll soul

1.

2.

3.

4.

5.

Since Buddhistpunk's birth in 1999 out of the union of a western aesthetic edge and artisan tropical heat, Buddhistpunk remains essentially the same small team that runs the London and Bali studios today.

The brand is headed up by label founder Rupert Meaker and designer Adam Entwisle.

2007 saw the well known counter culture label taking more steps to grow into the alternative fashion house that it set out to be, a David amongst the Goliaths, by subdividing the label into two specialist labels – Buddhistpunk by Adam Entwisle and House of the Gods.

House of the Gods was established to take advantage of the rock 'n' roll relationships that Buddhistpunk has built up since it was founded.

Buddhistpunk has collaborated both professionally and privately, whether for the stage, tour merchandise, publicity or their own personal wardrobes, with artists as diverse as Schooly D, The Prodigy, The Gossip, Gary Numan, The Rolling Stones, Blondie, Guns N' Roses, Aerosmith, Kylie, Britney, U2, Ian Astbury, Iggy Pop, The Doors, Pink Floyd, Roxy Music, Run DMC, David Bowie, The Police and many more.

Buddhistpunk is heavily print based and shares a natural aesthetic with rock 'n' roll, the spirit of being in the moment, of mixing pop culture iconography with the now, and is possibly the most integrated fashion house within the rock 'n' roll industry.

House of the Gods continues in the great tradition of rock 'n' roll garments and band tees which embody the spirit of some of the world's favourite artists, and was launched to specialise in design driven rock 'n' roll fashion, building on Buddhistpunk's heritage of printed and hand worked jersey collections.

With House of the Gods filling this role, Buddhistpunk by Adam Entwisle – men's and women's ready to wear – allows you to forget all that you thought Buddhistpunk was. Buddhistpunk by Adam Entwisle will express the true essence of the cult label, of authentic uptown meets downtown, highbrow meets lowbrow, high fashion meets pop culture.

Adam has helped creatively direct Buddhistpunk since 2002 and, with Buddhistpunk by Adam Entwisle, will be able to build on his high fashion reputation under the Buddhistpunk label – continuing a true fashion path, following in the tradition of the best known maverick labels.

Also new for 2007 was Buddhistpunk's partnership with L.E.N.Y (Limited Edition New York), launched in Spring/Summer 2007 at the world renowned Colette in Paris. L.E.N.Y is a seasonal co-celebrity designed label raising money for the environment – celebrity collaboration for a good cause, presently Al Gore's The Climate Project. Twelve celebrities including Kate Moss, Gwyneth Paltrow, Helena Christensen, Christy Turlington, Carine Roitfeld, Diane von Furstenberg and Ines van Lamsweerde/Vinoodh Matadin, each designed a unique t-shirt which Buddhistpunk handmade in a limited edition of 500 each and sold through some of the world's leading stores such as Corso Cuomo 10, Dover Street Market, Harvey Nichols, Isetan and Lane Crawford – to mention but a few.

For Autumn/Winter 2007, Buddhistpunk partners with L.E.N.Y again, making chic tote bags in collaboration with the 12 celebrities, as well as new limited edition t-shirts – one for each of the 12 new fashion icons who will be to helping to further increase awareness of The Climate Project and raise more funds.

Buddhistpunk Records is also moving from strength to strength after the success of Mattafix's first album 'Signs of a Struggle'; Mattafix are releasing their second album 'Rhythms and Hymns' in November 2007. Their new single 'Living' is also being used in the campaign to raise awareness of the war torn area of Darfur, with special cover art by world renowned artist Chris Ofili. Buddhistpunk Records has also recently signed the new talents The Ghost Frequency and Edwina Johnson.

Buddhistpunk aims to offer a considered independent alternative for the individual, in an ever more corporate world.

Canon
A photographic memory for innovation and style

050

From modest beginnings – a handful of employees and a burning passion – it didn't take long for Canon, celebrating its 70th anniversary in 2007, to become a world-renowned camera manufacturer.

The origins of its success remain unchanged: the passion of its early years and technological expertise amassed over decades.

Canon is now a world leader in photographic and imaging technology and has created several iconic brands including EOS, IXUS and PowerShot cameras, PIXMA and SELPHY printers, and some of the highest quality HD camcorders. The brand's digital compact cameras boast cutting-edge technologies and are the epitome of sleek, stylish design – as seen in the multi award-winning IXUS range, which celebrated its 10th anniversary in 2006 and included the first ever camera to be featured in London's Design Museum.

Canon's number one position in the European Digital Camera (digital compact and digital SLR combined) segment was recently confirmed by leading global market research organisation, GfK – the fifth consecutive year that the brand has achieved this ranking.

Part of Canon's enduring success lies in its ethos of cultivating existing technologies whilst developing and introducing innovative new products. In 2006, Canon's considerable investment in research and development (around eight per cent of global turnover is invested annually) resulted in 2,385

patents being filed. This success owes much to the brand's corporate philosophy of 'kyosei' – living and working together for the common good.

Fashion is a good fit for the Canon brand with many of its products being used across the industry at all levels, ranging from the EOS family of SLR cameras, which celebrates its 20th anniversary in 2007 to multi-format printers.

In celebration of Canon's second year as sponsor of London, Paris and Milan Fashion Weeks, and to mark Canon Europe's 50th anniversary, a major new European project across 17 countries was launched in 2007 – the 'We Speak Image' fashion campaign. For the project, Canon recruited British fashion designer Matthew Williamson, along with 16 other leading fashion designers from across Europe, to create a series of unique collections that captured the essence of their country, inspired by images taken by their fellow countrymen.

Furthermore, members of the public were invited to upload their most creative and iconic images, which represented the spirit of their nation, to a dedicated website. Canon made a donation to Red Cross Societies across Europe for each image uploaded. The most popular images, as voted for by the public, were then used by the fashion designers involved to inspire the 'national' fashion collection, created with the help of Canon's state-of-the-art imaging equipment. The resulting garments were showcased at London, Milan and Paris Fashion Weeks and made available for public viewing via installations and events across Europe.

A collaboration to support the tagging and tracking of individual polar bears in the Arctic region was also announced by Canon and WWF, the global conservation organisation, in 2007.

Building on Canon's long term support of WWF as a Conservation Partner since 1998, the new agreement ensures an increase in the number of polar bears tagged in 2007 into 2008, enabling WWF to significantly increase the amount of valuable scientific information it can collect on polar bears.

Chanel

Luxury is
when the
inside is as
beautiful as
the outside

052

chanel.com

CoolBrands 2007/08

Once in a while a visionary comes along whose influence leaves a defining and lasting impression. Gabrielle 'Coco' Chanel shaped and styled 20th century fashion through a creative tour-de-force, imparting along the way her legacy of modernity and chic.

Born in 1883, Gabrielle's early years remain shrouded in mystery. An orphan from birth, she was re-invented aged 25 as Coco, a popular singer in the garrison town of Moulins. It was from this point onwards that the chanteuse and accomplished equestrian started to build on the name she had established for herself.

Coco's first notable foray into the world of fashion came as a milliner in 1910. While the understated elegance of her hats left little impression on the fussily adorned ladies of the Belle Epoque, Coco remained undeterred, famously declaring that: "One could never be too modern." This philosophy of discretion over ostentation remains one of the brand's underlying principles, personified through Coco who – in flouting society's conventions, in both the way she dressed and how she lived her life – became her own best model and publicist.

It was during the upheaval of World War I that Coco's avant-garde approach really began to get her noticed. She became notorious for plundering men's wardrobes for ideas which she used to create unconventional fashions; deconstructing prevalent styles of the time. The results: stunning creations such as the sailor sweater and blazers that were to become enduring classic Chanel designs.

Coco's capriciousness led to the creation of its signature Chanel No. 5 perfume in 1921. The task, charged to legendary parfumeur Ernest Beaux, was to come up with something that reflected her personality: abstract and unique. The scent was the first to be sold worldwide and the first to display a pared-down style of packaging that immediately set it apart from the gaudy, feminine vials favoured by the 1920s fashionable set. Every detail – from the hexagonal stopper (a shape sourced from the Place Vendome which Coco's Paris suite overlooked) to the subtle typography – was a triumph to the contemporary appeal of the brand. The bottle has since acquired iconic status; being designated a 20th century design classic. In an attempt to ensure the scent's timeless quality the House of Chanel is now the main grower of may rose and jasmine (two key ingredients) in Grasse.

In 1983, 12 years after Coco's death, maverick designer Karl Lagerfeld took over as artistic director of Chanel;

a gamble which has paid off. His witty creations pay tribute to the brand's classic designs while reacting intuitively to changing times. Despite this change in direction the definitive Chanel suit – comprising of knee length skirt, boxy jacket, gold buttons and trim – has withstood the fads of modern times, remaining as popular today as ever. While Chanel is perhaps better known for its clothes, perfume and handbags it continues to develop a growing range of accessories, including jewellery, shoes and wallets. All are instantly recognisable thanks to the brand's distinctive logo – an overlocking double C, representing its founder's initials (Coco Chanel) – and the quality of workmanship that denotes luxury.

Chanel's belief that beauty should not be masked by frippery is perhaps nowhere more apparent than through its most famous asset – the little black dress. Always the fashion editor's favourite, now a 'must have' in every woman's wardrobe, the underlying philosophy is simple: classic, elegant design equals sexy perfection.

Coco Chanel was fashion's first problem solver; audacious, creative as well as independent. Today the brand retains the quintessential characteristics of its 'Grande Mademoiselle'.

Cobra Beer
Inspiration, Innovation, Ingenuity. In bottles.

054

Bangalore, India. 1989. A Cambridge law graduate named Karan Bilimoria has just launched Cobra, a premium beer specially brewed to be extra smooth and less gassy.

Karan plans to export it to the UK. He has £20,000 of student debt and no experience. He is launching a new brand in the world's most competitive beer market. Oh, and a recession has just started. It's going to be an interesting journey.

Eighteen years on and Cobra has come a long way. Geographically it's been quite a trip, with the beer being exported to 50 countries around the world. The company has also travelled far since those lean early days, becoming one of the UK's fastest growing beer brands. Cobra's hallmark throughout has been innovation, and a drive to do things differently. From telling the Cobra story with embossed icons on their bottles right through to their CobraVision short film competition, Cobra is a brand that thrives on being that little bit exceptional.

Nowhere is Cobra's drive to innovate more evident though than in its products. The original premium beer was itself exceptional, with less gas than regular lagers, and over the past few years Cobra has added no fewer than four new products to its portfolio. Cobra 0.0% alcohol-free and Cobra Lower Cal came first, followed by King Cobra – the world's first double-fermented lager. Befitting such a special bottle-conditioned beer, it is even packaged in elegant Champagne-style bottles. The most recent addition to the Cobra family is Cobra Bite, an exotic range of fruit-flavoured beers with 100 per cent natural

fruit extracts, including blood orange, sweet lime, apple and lemongrass.

Cobra's reach extends beyond its award-winning packaging and products. Its heavyweight through-the-line 'Unusual thing, excellence' campaign launched at the end of 2006, targeting discerning lager drinkers with Cobra's biggest ever national television campaign, The Lift.

In fact, Cobra has been making its presence felt on TV screens since 2005, with its CobraVision short film competition. Aspiring filmmakers are invited to submit their 50-second short films, with the best being shown before blockbuster movies on itv4. The initiative gives young filmmakers the chance to put their work in front of an audience of millions on national television, and is already working in association with a range of film partners and film festivals including Edinburgh, Bristol Encounters and Raindance. Moving from the small screen to the big screen, Cobra has recently had product placements in the films Hot Fuzz and The Hitchhiker's Guide to the Galaxy.

Cobra's association with the UK film industry through CobraVision has proved a fruitful one, increasing the visibility of the brand hugely. Cobra now counts exclusive London venues such as the Kingly Club and Leicester Square No. 1 among its list of prestigious accounts. It brews under license in five different

countries including India and the UK, and has offices in London, Mumbai, New York and Cape Town.

Add to this a trophy cabinet that includes more gold medals from the Monde Selection Awards for two years running than any other beer brand – and you have a noteworthy success in a notoriously tough industry.

When Karan Bilimoria poured the first Cobra in Bangalore, back in 1989, he had all the odds stacked against him but he had a mission, and he's stuck to it to this day: to brew the finest ever India beer and to make it a global beer brand. It looks like Karan and Cobra are well on their way.

Dazed & Confused
Off line and online,
never toeing the line.

056

dazeddigital.com

CoolBrands 2007/08

Dazed & Confused stands for agenda-setting editorial, world-beating fashion, brilliant photography and illustration, unrivalled music and film coverage, headline-grabbing events. But above all, it's still proud to be independent.

With distribution in over 40 countries and admirers and imitators across the globe, Dazed & Confused has come a long way since its first steps in the early 1990s.

Dazed Digital, now one year old, is bringing that same cutting-edge and ground-breaking ethos to the web. The world's first Ideas Sharing Network, Dazed Digital posts exclusive video interviews, live footage of tomorrow's music stars, behind-the-scenes fashion reportage, and exclusive features above and beyond what is in the magazine, all alongside daily blogs and submissions from its extended global network of writers, photographers, artists, and activists. Dazed has also taken its long-established tradition of nurturing and supporting new talent to the next level in the Rise section of Dazed Digital, where new talent in music, illustration, fashion and photography is profiled by Dazed's in-house creatives, with a special guest judge each month.

Innovative one-off projects already undertaken on Dazed Digital include a 24-hour non-stop live webcast of film and photography for World Aids Day on 1st December 2006, and Wanted, a digital 'outsider' exhibition that has to date received over 3,000 submissions from independent artists.

Founded by prodigious photographer Rankin and writer and cultural enthusiast Jefferson Hack, the brand takes its name (and freewheeling spirit) from the classic Led Zeppelin song, Dazed & Confused, starting life as a limited-run fold-out poster in 1992. Cover stars in those early days included PJ Harvey, Damien Hirst, Richard Ashcroft, Chloe Sevigny, Jarvis Cocker, Robert Carlyle, Kate Moss and Milla Jovovich. It was during this time that Dazed & Confused cemented its growing international reputation for daring to extend its editorial remit beyond fashion, music and film, not just to include art and literature, but to tackle local and international social and political themes.

With its fashion, photography and art content long established as some of the best in the world, in recent years Dazed has brought its music and film editorial up to similarly world-beating standards with a long list of UK and world firsts, including the likes of Eminem, The Libertines, Pharrell Williams and Alicia Keys. Under its current editors Nicki Bidder and Rod Stanley, recent cover exclusives have included The White Stripes, Maggie Gyllenhaal, Bloc Party, Zooey Deschanel, Sofia Coppola, Justin Timberlake, the Yeah Yeah Yeahs and Selma Blair.

The magazine's strong music association has also seen the Dazed & Confused brand extended to high profile live

DAZED DIGITAL

concerts, such as this year's War Child benefit at the London club Koko, which featured upcoming stars the Noisettes, Metronomy, Friendly Fires, and Late of the Pier. Dazed also recently launched its own monthly club night DZD, footage from which can be seen on Dazed Digital, including one of Kate Nash's earliest live sets, and Paris dance sensations Justice playing a surprise set. Dazed Digital has also hosted free label mixes from uber-hip Kitsune, Mad Decent and White Heat.

Today, still 100 per cent independent in ownership and in spirit, Dazed & Confused is perhaps the most influential monthly magazine in the world. Far from resting on its reputation, Dazed Digital is now pushing the brand's taste and influence into new areas, bringing it to life in more ways than ever, and engaging a new generation of switched-on, intelligent, aware and influential individuals.

Decléor
Revealing the pure essence of nature

058

Calling on centuries of knowledge in the ancient healing art of aromatherapy, Decléor has spent 30 years combining the purest, most potent natural ingredients with a unique holistic approach.

As the original and pioneering experts in Aroma-skincare, Decléor has continued to revolutionise and dominate the luxury aromatherapy skincare market.

As a brand Decléor focuses on rebalancing the mind, body and spirit, treating not just physical symptoms but every aspect of peoples' day-to-day lives. Decléor's range of products and treatments are not only beneficial for soothing, healing and moisturising but can also stimulate the olfactory senses, influencing the way the body feels and responds to stress.

Research and innovation play an important role at Decléor. International research laboratories in France, Japan and the US provide specialist insight into the benefits of essential oils on the skin and psyche; skin knowledge is translated into the brand's comprehensive range of aromatherapy and phytotherapy products. Uniting science with nature enables the development of increasingly effective cosmetic formulas, all adhering to two golden rules: nothing is synthetic and nothing is tested on animals.

Over the years, aromatherapy has proved itself to be a tangible science that uses the most active extracts of aromatic plants, the essential oils, to create effective skincare solutions. Essential oils have many varying properties, and once expertly blended can help to regulate each of the skin's basic functions: hydration, sebum excretion, stimulating cell renewal and defending against internal or external aggressors. Decléor ensures that only the purest essential oils are used in its Aromessences™, each sourced from quality producers worldwide – guaranteeing quality and effective results time-after-time.

The key to the brand's success lies in the Aromessence™, a powerful cocktail of essential oil concentrates that are 100 per cent pure, natural, active and preservative-free. Each of these carefully blended aromatic essences, developed for use on either face or body, has a natural affinity with the skin and penetrates easily and deeply where it is dispersed, leaving no oily residue.

Decléor's entire beauty philosophy is based on a simple yet effective two-fold system called the 'Aroma-Duo Concept', in which the Aromessences™' play an important role; that of acting as a natural beauty 'booster' when used in conjunction with a phytotherapy product. Each Aromessence™ and phytotherapy product is developed to correspond to a particular skincare 'prescription', achieving optimum results on all skin types; it is proven that using the duo concept dramatically improves results on both the face and body by up to 33 per cent.

Decléor's professional roots have long been associated with luxurious but highly effective treatments – designed to work in harmony with today's lifestyles, whilst ensuring that all skin types are provided with tailor made treatments to suit the individual.

Starting with massage techniques that centre around the nervous system and meridians, every Decléor treatment begins with a unique back diagnostic massage where a trained specialist uses pure Aromessences™ to aid drainage and promote a deep sense of relaxation. This diagnostic massage enables the therapist to assess a client's general condition and skin health in order to assimilate the correct Aromessences™ and professional concentrates for treatment. Each individual treatment – from facials to slimming, firming and relaxation – reinforces the Decléor philosophy of treating a person as a 'whole'.

Decleor is recognised around the world as the trusted expert and innovator in premium aromatherapy skincare, providing luxurious aromatherapy products and treatments for the face and body, revealing the pure essence of nature.

De'Longhi
Passionate,
stylish Italian
design

060

Innovation has always been the life-blood of De'Longhi. Italian to the core, its commitment to quality and style has kept it at the forefront of contemporary design for more than 100 years.

De'Longhi's heritage is firmly rooted in domestic appliances, originating as a component manufacturer in Treviso, near Venice. The family run business – whose craftsman's workshop became a small appliance company back in the 1950s – had, by the 1970s, launched its inaugural range of branded goods; portable electric radiators.

In the kitchen, De'Longhi revolutionised the marketplace with the launch of products such as the rotofryer – a deep fryer with a rotating basket and patented oil drain hose – and the fully automatic, bean-to-cup Magnifica and PrimaDonna coffee maker ranges, complete with patented 'single touch' espresso and cappuccino functions. Each range fuelled organic growth in new areas, eventually driving further diversification of the brand through notable acquisitions such as Simac Vetrella in 1989, and Kenwood in 2001.

It was in 1986, that De'Longhi introduced the pioneering concept of portable air conditioning to the market; the 'Pinguino' range becoming synonymous with home air conditioning. Today De'Longhi remains the leading global brand in this category.

De'Longhi's marketing and communication strategy reflects the brand's core values: Italian and 'different'. De'Longhi is the only Italian brand to focus solely on domestic coffee making gadgetry for the UK market, imparting the best of its 'espresso know-how'. It was the first brand to advertise coffee makers on television, its series of stylish ads in 2002 credited with driving the home coffee making market. De'Longhi has effectively doubled its 'coolness quotient' in 2007 by choosing Alfa Romeo as an official coffee partner – a brand also renowned for its Italian heritage and design.

The brand's success is embedded in its fundamental values. De'Longhi design has a definitive style that renders products instantly recognisable. Unique and unconventional, the brand philosophy is based on delivering the best in terms of style, performance, efficiency and quality. In order to facilitate the brand's competitive edge and maintain its market position, De'Longhi invests in state-of-the-art research and design facilities. Through pitching itself as a 'helpful' brand it continues to field resources into help-at-hand guides, product helplines and increase overall website accessibility. Product quality and reliability remain integral to De'Longhi's core values and are enforced by rigorous testing at its Italian production sites.

Awards won by De'longhi reinforce the brand's core values. For example, recognition for 'stand innovation' at consumer exhibitions such as the Good Food Show, at Birmingham's NEC – where a four metre high Argento toaster featured at its hub. In 2006, De'Longhi was the only brand of espresso coffee maker awarded the Good Housekeeping Institute seal of approval – this has been re-approved for 2007.

Owner and founder of the De'Longhi Group, Giuseppe De'Longhi, is very much at the core of the organisation; from major acquisitions through to product design and marketing. His son Fabio, who holds the post of Group CEO, is similarly involved across most facets of the business. It's frequently said that were you to cut a De'Longhi employee in half they would be blue and white (like the logo)… a testament to the brand. From the top down, De'Longhi engenders a level of loyalty and enthusiasm in its employees, a definitive pride in the brand.

Be it products, marketing or simply making domestic life easier, De'Longhi is a brand driven by innovation and a focus on customers' quality of life. Through continued development, investment and seminal design it has its sights set clearly and firmly on the future.

Dermalogica
The science
of healthy skin

ogica®

International Dermal Institute

062

dermalogica

Dermalogica believes that skin care is not about beauty; nor is it about pampering, luxury, indulgence or glamour but, like taking care of your teeth, a health necessity.

These are the underlying principles behind The International Dermal Institute, founded in Los Angeles in 1983 by Jane and Raymond Wurwand. The mission was simple: to educate and elevate the status of skin care professionals and, in doing so, set an industry standard. Jane – who had nurtured this vision since sweeping floors at a Poole beauty salon during her teens – saw The International Dermal Institute grow into the largest postgraduate training centre of its kind in the world. It now has 40 fully owned International Dermal Institute training centres worldwide, offering an ongoing forum for research and education in skin therapy.

Once The International Dermal Institute was up and running it was just a matter of time before a product line followed. The idea was to develop a product free from the common irritants that led to skin sensitisation, which could be recommended by professional skin therapists with the same confidence as a doctor would prescribe medicine. Despite being repeatedly told that "it couldn't be done", the Dermalogica brand was launched in 1986 and, within three years, became a leading professional skin therapy product, advocating the importance of maintaining healthy skin.

These first few Dermalogica formulas are still bestsellers. Over the years – despite expansion and diversification – the brand has remained loyal to its founding vision:

intelligent products for intelligent consumers. Through word of mouth it has built up a sizable cult following among celebrities, industry specialists and Hollywood makeup artists.

All Dermalogica products are researched and developed by The International Dermal Institute. By utilising the expertise of the school's worldwide network of educators the brand is able to continually research and explore new ingredients, techniques and trends; predicting emerging trends is key to continued innovation.

The newly opened Dermalogica Store in London's Kensington offers a fresh approach to retail therapy, by way of a skin treatment centre, shopping outlet and education facility – all under one roof. Designed for today's generation of conscientious consumers (who like to try before they buy), The Dermalogica Store includes a specialist skin treatment room, product pool and Skin Barsm (skin products and herbal teas on tap) where customers can indulge in free mini face treatments 'prescribed' by a Dermalogica skin therapist. The new store reinforces the brand's commitment to education by offering fun, interactive classes where customers can experience Dermalogica products first-hand while simultaneously learning about the science of skincare.

At the core of Dermalogica's philosophy lies the belief that skin evolves throughout a lifetime. Therapists are therefore trained to recognise and interpret these changing conditions using Face Mapping® – Dermalogica's unique method of skin analysis. The brand's emphasis on education and information is what sets it apart from its competitors, this and its non-compromising stance in support of its therapists.

Dermalogica's approach has always been – and remains – bold, with a strong

commitment to creating no-nonsense products. Twenty one years on, its core values of innovation, function and education have remained integral to its brand identity. However, commitment to its foundations doesn't imply inertia. On the contrary, a brand's success depends on progression and momentum – constantly evolving while maintaining credibility. Dermalogica's research background enables it to anticipate industry trends and maintain its key position at the forefront of new developments in skin therapy.

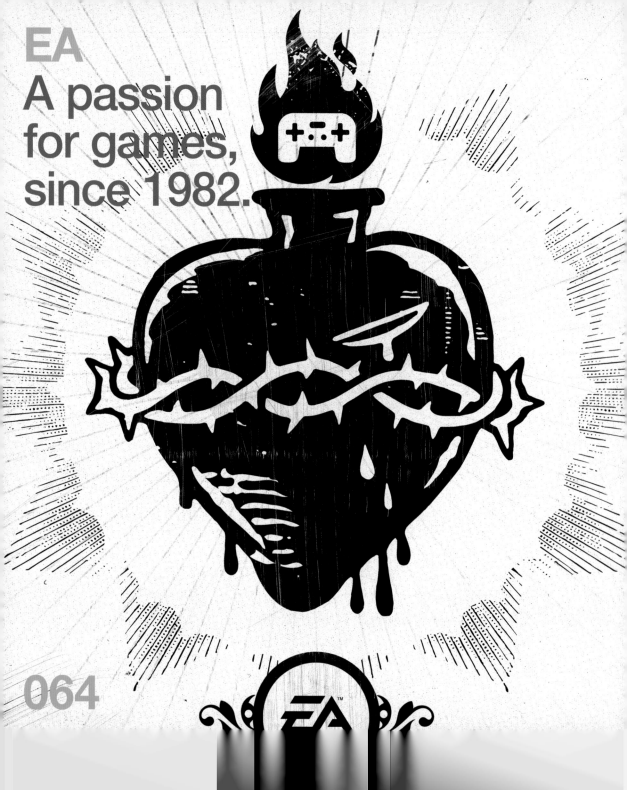

EA

A passion
for games,
since 1982.

064

It's been emotional. "The work we publish will be work that appeals to the imagination... They will be programs that encourage exploration, discovery, curiosity and creativity." – Excerpt from original EA manifesto, 1982.

In 1982, a group of visionaries founded Electronic Arts (EA) to harness the potential of the fledgling personal computer while embracing a radically different way of thinking about it. The central idea behind their vision was a question that would influence EA's direction for the next quarter of a century: Can a computer make you cry?

EA believed that electronic artistry would one day rival that of other creative industries, such as film-making. They were convinced that when computers could technologically support artists' ideas, innovation and passion, games would begin to engage players on an emotional level. Twenty five years later, that vision seems quite prophetic.

We are in the midst of an interactive, online revolution – and companies like EA are leading the charge. Interactive entertainment is now mainstream and players' experiences have drastically changed. They're no longer 'on rails', completing a series of missions in a prescribed order. Today EA enables players to take control of the virtual worlds – giving them the tools to tell their own stories, in their own styles, and to shape their own worlds. Perhaps just as importantly, players can also share their experiences with an ever-expanding community.

With this liberating power to express, players no longer just play: they create, explore, discover and connect – feeding their curiosity and imagination and tapping into the artist within. Interactivity emotionally connects players to characters and virtual worlds because when we create something, we naturally become attached to it – and are then more prone to laugh, fall in love, gasp in amazement, quake in fear and yes, even cry.

These days we hear a lot about 'user-generated-content' and every brand strives to be interactive, entertaining and a part of this trend. EA stands out because this idea isn't new to the brand. It's been part of its vision since the company's inception and EA has consistently provided us with tools that encourage us to create.

The EA logo, recognised as a stamp of quality throughout the world, now embraces this idea of creativity as well. Recently EA initiated a new, flexible approach, incorporating the spirit of each game and franchise into variations of its logo. As a result, the EA brand is now fully integrated into the creative experience itself.

With an all-star line-up of the world's best-loved brands and franchises including EA SPORTS, The Sims, SimCity, Medal of Honor, FIFA and Tiger Woods, a new division devoted to casual gaming, cutting-edge IP and a host of other new titles (Spore, Skate, Rock Band, Boogie and more) on the horizon, EA is positioning itself to continue to advance its engaging vision.

In 2007, 25 years after EA's foundation, it is still driven by its passion for games and by a consistent pursuit to further the possibilities of interactive entertainment – just as it was in its 1982 manifesto in which it proclaimed it was "an association of electronic artists united by a common goal: to fulfil the enormous promise of interactive entertainment". Wherever the future of interactive entertainment takes us, we expect EA to be leading the way.

Eden Project
Vibrant, entertaining,
informative and
inspiring

066

While its futuristic covered biomes may have gained plenty of column inches, the Eden Project has proved itself to be much more than just a green theme park.

Building the Eden Project as a landmark was always part of the wider strategy: to create an unforgettable experience in a breathtaking location; a living theatre of plants and people encased in extraordinary architecture. Through attracting a cross section of visitors in high numbers, its primary intention was to encourage the exploration of man's evolving relationship with, and dependence on plants.

The Eden Project opened fully to the public on 17th March 2001, but the story began when Cornish architect Jonathan Ball worked alongside Tim Smit, co-founding the project, before handing over to the recently knighted Sir Nicholas Grimshaw.

Their faith in Eden's vision was contagious; two construction companies – Sir Robert and Alfred McAlpine – were persuaded to work for 18 months without a fee or contract. This unprecedented and unorthodox arrangement was compounded when the businesses also agreed to loan Eden money towards completion, with repayment dependent on the Project's success. As it turned out, a calculated risk; to date over seven million visitors have passed through Eden's doors, making it one of the top five paid for visitor attractions in the UK and the main tourist attraction in the South West.

Its overwhelming success has helped it to win an array of significant awards in its short history. These have included Eden

Project's domination of the Group Travel Awards – since opening, it has amassed three wins and three runners-up ratings. In 2001, it was voted as a BT Vision Top 100 Company, then in 2003, its new product marketing was recognised at the CIM/Marketing Week Marketing Effectiveness Awards; it received a Visit Britain Gold as well as a Silver award for tourism marketing; and came third in Radio 4 Today Programme's 'Seven Wonders of Britain' vote. More recently, at the 2005 Cornwall Tourism Awards, A Time of Gifts was recognised with a Marketing Initiative award.

The Eden Project's main focus is education – at all levels. The biomes and visual displays are not only impressive but provide the foundation for a superior scientific and learning institution, dedicated to exploring issues surrounding sustainable development. Eden's education centre, The Core, emphasises its commitment to learning in the broadest sense; the thought-provoking exhibits open to everyone, not just students, scientists and academics.

As with education, the arts, in their broadest sense, are fundamental to Eden with artistic pieces nestling amongst the greenery. Eden has also played host to some groundbreaking events such as Live 8 Africa Calling and its increasingly popular Eden Sessions – outdoor summer gigs featuring big-name acts such as Amy Winehouse, Lily Allen, Basement Jaxx and Brian Wilson.

Story-telling is Eden's lifeblood, with guides and performers increasing awareness with humour and, invariably, a great deal of wisdom. Conversations, performances and interaction aim to both entertain and educate. Themed seasons such as Bulb Mania in spring, A Time of Gifts in winter and Jungle Nights in the summer are less a marketing ploy and more a way of

demonstrating visually that, like its plants, the Eden Project continues to evolve.

The Edge represents the next evolution of Eden. With its roots firmly entrenched in the Project's original ambition to have a biome focusing on the desert regions of the world, it will concentrate on the topical challenges of water use and water security, energy use and energy security as well as climate change. The building will be a landmark construction in the tradition that Eden is renowned for – a dynamic fusion of architecture, technology, science and the arts.

The Eden Project is a showcase that raises many questions and puts forward some of the answers. It is not worthy, over-serious or guilt-ridden; nor does it preach. It is about education and communication with major environmental issues of the day presented in an engaging, involving, and often humorous, way. Above all, the Eden Project takes a fresh look at our world and our place within it.

first direct
Create a bank around you

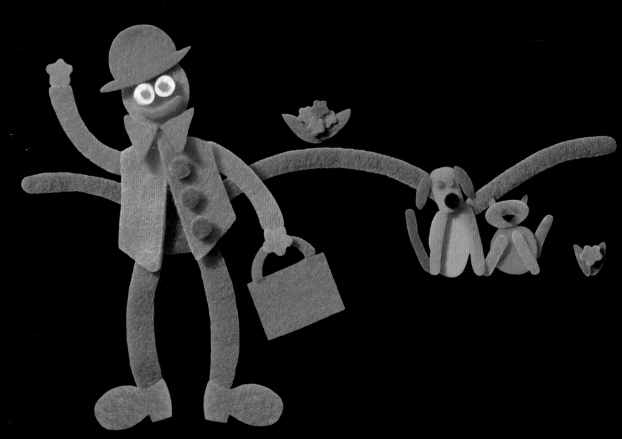

firstdirect.com

CoolBrands 2007/08

first direct was the pioneer of direct banking in the UK. While many competitors have imitated this formula, first direct remains an innovator, building on its reputation as the bank where people matter most.

The banking market has changed dramatically since first direct launched in 1989. While many consumers have become disillusioned with their banks, first direct has maintained a loyal customer base, who ensure that it remains the UK's most recommended bank (Source: First Response Survey, Q4 2006).

Through a combination of effective technology and unexpected human touches, first direct makes its customers' lives a little easier, and their banking a little less boring.

With its award-winning online banking service, customers can carry out their banking at the touch of a button. Or if they prefer to talk, first direct's telephone staff are available 24 hours a day, 365 days a year. first direct promises that customers will always get straight through to a real person, every time they call. There is no automation – just a friendly, helpful person in Leeds or Lanarkshire.

Indeed, whenever they communicate with their bank – via the internet, text message and telephone banking, or the many other ways that first direct communicates with its customers – they can expect to be treated in a friendly, open and adult-to-adult way.

This customer focus manifests itself in the ongoing development of new ways for first direct to engage with its customers and to take the hassle out of their banking. For example, Internet Banking Plus, launched in 2004, makes customers' lives easier by allowing them to view all of their online accounts in one place.

More recently, first direct trialled the myfd.mobi site, giving customers access to a range of features and services through their mobile phones. This included the facility to video-call the bank, allowing customers to speak to first direct face-to-face for the first time.

March 2007 saw the launch of first direct interactive, a website featuring advice and information tailored to its customers' needs. As well as information about the brand and its products, the website includes a series of podcasts, produced in association with the Financial Times, on topics such as financial family planning and making the most of ISA allowances.

The site also includes a 'virtual forest' encouraging customers to suppress their paper statements. For each customer who does this, first direct plants one tree in the virtual forest. For every 20 virtual trees, a real tree will be planted. Visitors can watch the virtual forest grow, and vote for where the real trees should be located.

During the summer of 2007, the first direct Magic Bus went on the road. The bus turned up at shows and events, giving out free gifts, and allowing both customers and non-customers the chance to experience first direct, first hand.

With initiatives such as these, first direct continues to find new ways to engage with its customers and to ensure that its customers just keep on recommending.

Fresh & Wild
Fun & friendly
Food & people

wholefoodsmarket.com

CoolBrands 2007/08

Who says organic food can't be fun? Not long ago it had a reputation for worthy dullness; a perception Fresh & Wild changed for good with its first London shop in 1998.

Fun is taken seriously at Fresh & Wild where shopping is seen as more of a pleasure than a necessity. The brand embraces its unconventional approach, from the individual look of its stores to its eclectic musical choices. Food sampling is also positively encouraged with breads, cheeses, chocolates and meat, all available to taste. This ongoing passion for sharing has helped Fresh & Wild become the UK's leading retailer of natural and organic food.

Fresh & Wild came about following the buyout of two former London health stores – Wild Oats and Freshlands. Founder, Hass Hassan, put his knowledge of informed natural food retailing (honed in the US) to good use generating a buzz with the opening of the brand's first store. It wasn't long before Fresh & Wild began to accrue retail awards for quality and innovation.

Further London-based Fresh & Wild outlets soon followed in Camden, Soho, Clapham Junction, the City, Notting Hill, and Stoke Newington, and, in 2003, the first store located outside the capital opened – in the Clifton area of Bristol. In 2004 Fresh & Wild joined forces with US company Whole Foods Market, the world's largest natural and organic retailer and in 2007 opened its 80,000 sq ft flagship store on Kensington High Street.

The original vision for Fresh & Wild was simple: to focus on providing the highest quality natural products, free from nasties such as artificial colourings, flavourings, preservatives and hydrogenated fat. This vision hasn't changed; the brand's long-standing commitment to stringent quality standards remains a crucial element that helps to set it apart from other food retailers. By continuing to stock and sell only the highest quality natural and organic foods – and locally sourcing whenever possible – Fresh & Wild has stayed true to its founding principles.

Despite maintaining a high profile, Fresh & Wild do relatively little by way of external marketing and advertising, relying instead on community involvement, word-of-mouth recommendation, and store-based initiatives to promote the brand. This non-conformist approach fits in with its hands-on, decentralised style and enables individual store and team members to become more directly involved in the brand.

Staff are held in high regard at Fresh & Wild, with its continued success owing much to the collective energy and intelligence of team members. Passionate, informed, friendly and, above all, food-loving staff are seen as ideal ambassadors for the brand, reinforcing its ethos and showing the light-hearted side to organic produce.

Environmental issues have always been an important part of the brand's identity. Fresh & Wild's continued support of organic farmers and growers demonstrates its ongoing commitment to sustainable agriculture while at the same time contributing to developing the organic market. Environmental practices are ingrained in the brand's working culture with its policy of 'recycling, reusing, and reducing waste wherever and whenever' fundamental to decreasing its overall environmental impact.

Community responsibility is also high on Fresh & Wild's agenda, with each shop donating five per cent of their daily proceeds, four times a year, to a variety of community and non-profit organisations, including disadvantaged children, local shelters, funds, hospices and food banks. It's not only money that is donated; employees give their time willingly through voluntary work.

Since its inception Fresh & Wild has grown to become part of many people's daily life and routine, a place to meet up for coffee, shop and seek advice from a well-informed team.

Gaggia
Innovation blended with classic design

Gaggia is at the heart of café culture, with a range of machines that not only grace coffee shops and restaurants around the world, but also bring a bit of Italy into the home.

Modern coffee-making methods owe much to Achille Gaggia. Until 1938, when he patented the first modern machine, espresso relied on blasting coffee grounds with steam. Gaggia's ingenious invention forced water to flow over the grounds at high pressure, producing the 'crema', unique to espresso. It revolutionised the way that coffee was made.

Since 1947, when the company was founded, Gaggia has been renowned for making consistently high quality machines and is widely acknowledged as a leading authority within the industry; the distinctive red and white logo is associated globally with authentic Italian coffee. It was during the 1970s – a time when bar quality espresso was growing in popularity – that Gaggia produced its first domestic machine.

The Baby Gaggia helped to propel the brand to the forefront of the domestic machine market, a position it has retained since, despite robust competition.

To celebrate 30 years of the Baby, Gaggia has introduced five new versions of the machine. The range includes a variety of colours, finishes and features all based around the original model.

Gaggia prides itself on the use of cutting-edge technology combined with traditional design. By allowing its design and performance to speak for itself,

Gaggia has created an understated, yet highly effective, marketing strategy.

Coffee, like many commodities today, now comes in various manifestations to cater for a wide diversity of tastes from beans and ground form to pods and capsules. As such, this demands a wider variety of coffee machines. Gaggia is the only brand which manufactures machines in three categories – Traditional, Bean to Cup and Capsules – in both professional and home markets.

Capsules are a new innovation which offer a way of producing quality coffee, without the mess. Most traditional machines, while able to cope with ground coffee or pods could only, until recently, use capsules in closed systems (machines that take capsules from just one roaster). Gaggia's ethos of embracing change encouraged the brand to explore ways of combining an open coffee system with capsules, to extend consumer choice and enable customers to select precisely what went into each machine.

To meet this task it adapted two of its models with extraction capabilities that could best utilise the Caffitaly System. The capsules are structured to allow water to fully irrigate each individual grain, guaranteeing a consistent flow of high quality coffee. The optimum amount of finely ground coffee is vacuum-sealed into each disposable, ready-to-use capsule, in order to create a cup of genuine Italian espresso.

But for those who still prefer to grind their own coffee in the time honoured tradition – and Gaggia recognise that many do – the capsule system can be converted to accommodate loose coffee with a simple kit. These fit easily on to all Gaggia machines, irrespective of whether the machine is new or 30 years-old.

As a brand Gaggia continues to move forward. Initiatives such as the Caffe Academie – offering young people hands-on work experience and follow-on support within the coffee trade and related industries – demonstrate its commitment to development and evolution. The scheme has attracted attention from leading restaurants, such as Carluccio's and Pizza Express, who acknowledge the long term benefits of providing stimulating training opportunities, within the marketplace, for young people.

Gaggia epitomises outstanding design and continuing innovation and while it keeps on producing quality machines and accessories, the UK's growing love affair with coffee shows no sign of abating.

Gaydar.co.uk
The ultimate
gay personals
website

074

Eight years after Gaydar.co.uk and its associated urls were launched, the portal has created an unprecedented online gay and lesbian community which has grown to become the world's biggest online dating and social networking website.

When Gaydar.co.uk was first launched, it completely revolutionised the way gay men could date and socialise in a new, private space away from the usual bars and clubs. Today, many gay men and lesbian women now have Gaydar profiles, which they exchange as regularly as phone numbers. Furthermore, for thousands of isolated individuals who live in countries where homosexuality remains illegal or homophobia highly prevalent, Gaydar.co.uk is an invaluable lifeline that allows them to chat freely, confidentially and safely with like-minded people.

The entrepreneurs and business partners, Gary Frisch and Henry Badenhorst, conceived the service in 1999 because other available dating sites were too slow and laborious to use. Everything on Gaydar.co.uk was much quicker and less formal, with an easy to use interface and functionality. The service included a Who's Online page that told users who else was visiting the site at the same time, and enabled users to message each other instantly.

The portal grew rapidly, primarily through word of mouth, with membership rates increasing by 10 per cent month-on-month. By November 2000, it had 78,000 registered members, rising the following year to 220,000. Gaydar.co.uk has since amassed 4.12 million users in 160 countries, including the UK, Australia, South Africa, Spain, Italy, the Netherlands and Belgium – making it the portal with the greatest traffic worldwide amongst the gay community. On average, guests spent just over 41 minutes on Gaydar.co.uk in March 2007, 25 minutes longer than the average time spent on other dating sites that month (Source: Hitwise).

One of the principal reasons for Gaydar's success has been its unswerving commitment to its community. The ethos of the company is one of giving back to the community that created it, through the sponsorship of major international events such as Sydney Mardi Gras, EuroPride and the UK Pride Season as well as more grassroots support for bars and clubs. This has since been extended into sports sponsorship for London's 2007 international gay and lesbian tennis tournament, The Tennis London International Championships.

New brand extensions such as the female variant, GaydarGirls.com, have successfully expanded the footprint further. The launch of GaydarRadio five years ago means the brand now reaches more than 72 per cent of gay and lesbian traffic on the internet. The station reaches a monthly, predominantly male, audience of around 1.6 million listeners. Available nationally on Sky Channel 0158, globally online and on digital radio in London and the Sussex coast, GaydarRadio was crowned UK Digital Terrestrial Station of the Year at the prestigious 2007 Sony Radio Awards, Digital Radio Station of the Year at the 2007 Arqiva Commercial Radio Awards and was voted Best Radio Station by listeners at the BT Digital Music Awards 2006.

2007 is another year of ambitious expansion for parent company QSoft

Consulting, which owns and operates the portfolio. April saw the opening of Profile, a new joint venture with Vince Power Music Group, which now brings to life the virtual Gaydar.co.uk brand via a stylish new entertainment venue situated in the heart of London's Soho.

A new mobile dating service, GaydarMobile also launched, initially to Gaydar.co.uk's 1.1 million subscribers, with a view to rolling the service out across Australia and continental Europe. This was followed by the arrival of GaydarNation.com, an amalgamation of the male and female portals with GaydarRadio and the lifestyle website, Rainbow Network, into the world's biggest interactive lifestyle destination for gay and lesbian people and their friends. For advertisers wanting to reach this lucrative ABC1 audience, GaydarNation offers a cross platform one stop shop which captures the market at different times of the day and at different times in their lives.

Innovation, together with an innate understanding and close relationship with its audience, has propelled Gaydar.co.uk to its number one status as the destination of choice for gay, lesbian and gay friendly people. Just like its audience, the brand continues to embrace and drive change for the benefit of users everywhere.

Goldsmiths,
University of London
Freedom of thought
and expression

076

Goldsmiths is about the freedom to experiment, to think differently, to be an individual.

Goldsmiths has nearly 9,000 students from all over the world and is proud of its reputation in the arts and in design, but Goldsmiths is much more than an 'art school'. By breaking down traditional boundaries, and promoting freedom of thought and expression, it brings unique and creative approaches to all of its subjects. Goldsmiths offers a broad range of undergraduate, postgraduate, professional and general interest courses in the arts and humanities (art, design, drama, history, literature, media and communications, music, visual cultures); social sciences (anthropology, computing, psychology, sociology); and education.

Design student Alexander Holmes got to the heart of what makes Goldsmiths different when he said: "Unlike other universities, which might set a brief asking you to design a chair, at Goldsmiths you are encouraged to question why the object needs to exist in the first place. This combination of flexibility and strong theoretical underpinning was key to my decision to study at Goldsmiths."

One of its greatest strengths is 'interdisciplinarity' – the way in which people throughout the College work together to contribute new insights from other disciplines. Goldsmiths supports collaborations in a dazzling array of permutations: psychologists work with computer scientists, artists with cultural theorists, musicians with anthropologists. The result is ground-breaking, challenging research that puts Goldsmiths at the forefront of developments in fields such as creativity, culture, and digital technologies. As Miguel Andrés-Clavera, who is studying in the Goldsmiths Digital

Studios, says: "Here you can have breakfast with a postmodern painter, lunch with an algorithmic composer and a psychologist, and hang out with 'cyber performers' and art critics whilst talking about your own research."

Founded in 1891 to promote 'technical skill, knowledge, health and general well-being among men and women of the industrial, working and artisan classes', and part of the University of London since 1904, Goldsmiths is known for individuals who have made themselves heard in their respective fields. Such luminaries include: Lucian Freud, Mary Quant, Damien Hirst, Bridget Riley, Anthony Gormley, Malcolm McLaren, John Cale, Alex James, Graham Coxon, Corrie Corfield, Ian Rickson and Tessa Jowell MP.

Goldsmiths embraces development and in 2007 has introduced inspiring new courses like the MSc in Computer Games and Entertainment, and the MA in Geo-Sociology. Following this, 2008 will see the launch of a new Master's in Music, Mind and Brain – the only course of its kind in the world. Innovation isn't confined to the academic sphere: the 'scribble' on the stunning Ben Pimlott Building is now a feature of the South East London skyline – and there are plans for more new buildings, including

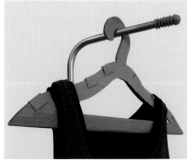

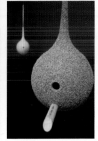

one for the Department of Media and Communications. By improving facilities and teaching spaces, Goldsmiths is ensuring that its environment continues to foster radical and creative thinking, underpinned by academic excellence and a commitment to providing opportunities for all.

By daring to be different, Goldsmiths offers not just a rigorous intellectual training, but a transformative experience of self-discovery.

Main image Geoff Wilson Additional images Anna Gover (top), David King (middle left), Nadine Jarvis (middle right), Natasja Mitcham (bottom)

Gü
Chocolate extremists with a good dollop of fun

8 CHOCOLATE BROWNIES MADE WITH 50% COCOA CHOCOLATE + PECAN NUTS

It was in Belgium, a country renowned for its chocolate heritage, that the seed was first sown for the artisan brand Gü.

James Averdieck had moved to Brussels with a leading dairy company in 1998, and while there he quickly became a convert to the art of Belgian gastronomy. James spotted a gap in the UK market – consumers were craving a high quality chocolate patisserie, to fit around their busy lifestyles.

In early 2002, James met with Rensow Patisserie, an upmarket supplier of quality artisinal puddings. The introduction was well timed for both parties; to capitalise on consumer trends and add value to the chilled pudding sector. Gü Chocolate Puds was finally launched by James Averdieck in May 2003, a joint venture with Rensow Patisserie.

Three products were initially introduced in Waitrose and Sainsbury's: Gü Hot Chocolate Soufflés, Gü Chocolate Truffle with Raspberry Compôte; and Gü Chocolate & Amaretto Truffle – all packaged in re-usable glass ramekins. In 2005, Gü Chocolate Puds launched a fruity little sister, Frü Fruity Puds, a range of premium chilled fruit-based desserts.

After the popularity of its early products, Gü's continued success was bolstered by its pacy product development, with 16 new products launching in 2007 – all meeting the Gü prerequisite of 'to-die-for products in sexy packaging'.

Gü expanded outside the UK in 2006 when it ventured into France and Begium – its chocolate souffles becoming a big hit in Paris and Brussels.

While Gü's popularity is very much built on quality and taste, brand identity also plays an important role. The name and identity were created by London branding agency Big Fish®; eye-catching packaging with a contemporary look and feel is designed to stand out, and traditional product descriptors have been spurned in favour of a playful language, with 'Gü-isms' on each pack describing individual products, illustrating that although the brand is serious about chocolate, it doesn't take itself too seriously. The logo remains simple, clear and recognisable, while the brand name conjures up gooey chocolate childhood memories.

Self-appointed 'Gü-meister', and founder James Averdieck, has built up a team of chocolate extremists, where product development happens at a grassroots level, involving all members of the small, young team. Fed by Fred – the hailed French development chef – the team has become adept at recognising brand opportunities and going for it.

Gü recognises that consumer tasting is key to its success so invests heavily in sampling. During the summer of 2007, it reached around 500,000 consumers through food shows, music and cultural events and a supermarket roadshow that roamed the country from Brighton to Manchester. Perhaps more significantly since June 2006, a Gü Pud has been served on all Virgin Atlantic flights, reaching over one million people in the first six-month period. An accompanying television campaign capitalised on this high profile status by reinforcing brand awareness.

As a brand Gü is about chocolate extremism with most Chocolate Puds produced in the UK using 53 per cent Belgian cocoa chocolate. While the original Gü Hot Chocolate Soufflé remains a favourite the brand has gone on to launch a raft of new products; from gü-ey brownies to decadent ice cream, all delivered with its trademark dollop of fun.

Gü Chocolate Puds and Frü Fruity Puds are the market leaders in the premium desserts sector with a brand value of £22 million – growing at 80 per cent year-on-year. Furthermore, the company was voted 'Best New Company' in the Sage Business Awards 2004, one of the 'Fifty to Watch' by Real Business in 2004, and won three Taste Awards during 2006. It just goes to show that the proof really is in the pudding.

Diptease?

We don't believe anyone can resist dipping their fruity bits in our new hot chocolate fondü. Made with 53% cocoa chocolate, served in a seductive black ceramic dish. If that's not enough, we're also offering ü the chance to win a naughty night in a five star hotel with a special friend. So, why not instantly see if ü have won at www.gupuds.com

H&M

A Swedish soul with a flare for affordable fashion.

Sixty years after Erling Persson opened the first 'Hennes' (Swedish for her's) shop in Västerås, Sweden – with a view to selling international high fashion at affordable prices – its brand ethos remains intact.

The first shop only sold women's clothes, but when Persson moved to Stockholm with expansion in mind he bought the premises of hunting store Mauritz Widforss, acquiring a stock of men's clothing in the process. Hennes became Hennes & Mauritz (H&M) and throughout the 1960s and 1970s expanded into northern Europe, adding children's wear and young fashion to the collection. H&M has continued its international expansion and today has more than 1,400 stores in 28 countries, including the 2007 opening of its first stores in Hong Kong and Shanghai, China.

The H&M product offer has also seen great expansion and now encompasses ranges for women, men, teenagers, children and babies as well as cosmetics and shoes.

Improvement, development and change dominate the company culture and its 60,000 staff are encouraged to resist the 'bureaucracy of big business' and hold on to the H&M mentality. H&M's head of design, Margareta van den Bosch, has built up the design department since her arrival in 1987. Today, there are around 100 designers, design assistants and pattern constructors in the design department working with its buyers. Van den Bosch strives to foster good relations with renowned design schools in Europe, the US and Australia,

recruiting many new designers fresh from school or college.

A global fashion brand, H&M is a pioneer of design collaborations with previous partnerships including international style and celebrity icons such as Viktor & Rolf, Stella McCartney, Karl Lagerfeld, Madonna and Kylie Minogue.

With this year's designer collaboration, H&M opens its doors to the world of Roberto Cavalli. The Italian designer will create a one-off collection for women and men exclusively for H&M. A designer to the stars, he regularly dresses international personalities such as Beyoncé, Gwyneth Paltrow, Charlize Theron, Jennifer Lopez, Sharon Stone, Gong Li, Victoria Beckham, Lenny Kravitz and Adrien Brody.

The 'Roberto Cavalli at H&M' collection will be available in approximately 200 selected H&M stores worldwide for a limited period of time, from November 2007.

H&M isn't just style without substance. It is very aware of how its clothes are made and has been using organic cotton for several years in selected babies' and children's garments. As the worldwide production of organic cotton begins to increase, H&M has now expanded its use of this material into its ladies', men's and younger ranges.

H&M recognises that designers can learn through their customers and encourages a two-way communication with them, with many (stylists in their own right) providing inspiration for staff. H&M, for its part, encourages customers to develop their own fashion identity; mixing seasonal trends with fashion basics, vintage and sports classics from its extensive product range. An important arena for H&M customer communication is via the shop, which formulates every

customer's shopping experience. The major purpose of each H&M store, besides offering the right product for each customer, is to create an attractive, comfortable environment where every customer feels at home.

The brand's advertising department works closely with external independent creative professionals. H&M adverts are largely identical irrespective of their intended market, but the media mix is adapted to meet local needs and conditions. H&M campaigns aim to generate consumer interest, and project a positive company image through a mix of looks and styles. Both are key elements to this fashionista.

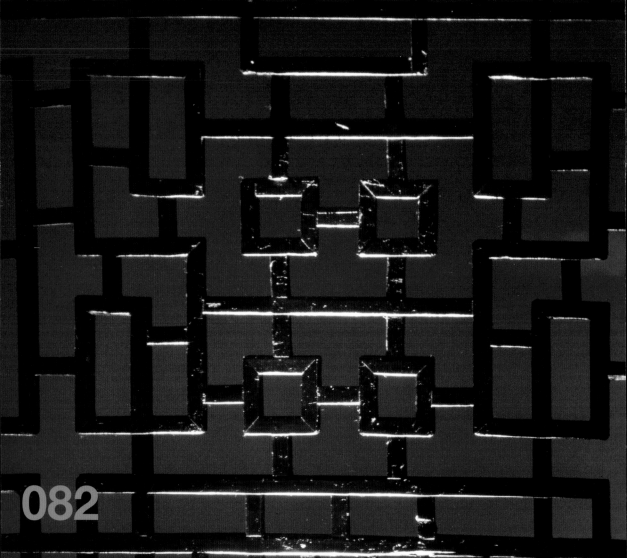

Hakkasan
Chinese cuisine in sensuous decadence

ha⊁kasan

At the turn of the millennium, acclaimed restaurateur Alan Yau read a review which said that London had no Chinese restaurants to rival those in Hong Kong and Singapore. He decided to change this situation.

From its modest exterior in a London backstreet, it is word of mouth that leads diners into the restaurant. The striking, decadent design fits Yau's original brief of 'bringing back the dragon'. It is the work of celebrated interior designer Christian Liaigre – otherwise know for the homes of Karl Lagerfeld and Calvin Klein as well as such design statements as New York's ultra-hip fashion palace, the Mercer Hotel.

The interior is divided into three distinct areas: a main dining room that seats 145; a lounge styled area; and a 16 metre long bar, made from dark-stained English Oak. The same dark wood has been used on the tables in sharp contrast to the lighter tones of blue glass and green slate surrounding the walls. A wall of sawn slate provides a dramatic background for nocturnal bar activity separated from the more tranquil setting of the dining area.

Oriental wooden screens (decorated with contemporary geometric designs) form a 'cage' around the main dining room, providing tantalizing glimpses of fellow diners as well as the bar and lounge beyond, thus lending an almost conspiratorial atmosphere. The kitchen, partially visible from the restaurant, generates a theatrical eloquence to the whole experience, with the chefs

becoming intrinsically part of the occasion rather than separate from it.

With detail being key to the overall success of the design, the lighting was put in the hands of leading technician Arnold Chan from Isometrix and the uniforms were created by leading fashion designer Hussein Chalayan.

Hakkasan has both style and substance. The Head Chef, Tong Chee Hwee, whose experience comes from the renowned Summer Pavilion Chinese restaurant at the Ritz Carlton in Singapore, brought his strong team with him, including sous chef and master Dim Sum chef. Together they create a modern authentic Cantonese menu, with dishes that have been modified slightly to retain their Chinese authenticity.

Hakkasan's reputation was sealed when it was awarded its first Michelin star in 2002 (which it has retained ever since), only one year after the restaurant opened, being at that time the only Chinese restaurant to have such an accolade. In the same year, it was also awarded 'outstanding contribution to London restaurants' at the Moët &

Chandon London Restaurant Awards. Every year since, Hakkasan has been bestowed with many awards including: Oriental Restaurant of the Year 2003 and 2004 by Carlton London Restaurant Awards; Number 30 within the Top 50 Restaurants in the World by Restaurant magazine in 2005; and Best London Chef for Tong Chee Hwee at the 2005 Tio Pepe/ITV London Restaurant Awards.

In 2006, Alan Yau was given the prestigious honour of being awarded an OBE for Contribution to the British Restaurant Industry.

Such success hasn't made Yau rest on his laurels – 2007 will see Hakkasan opening in Istanbul and Abu Dhabi, providing more first class Chinese eating emporiums.

Harman Kardon
Delighting audio
purists everywhere

Harman Kardon® stands for simple, beautiful entertainment technology and has taken a leading role in the creation and innovation of progressive technologies, providing audio products for the home, computer and automotive industries.

It was a love of music that drove Dr Sidney Harman to found Harman Kardon more than 50 years ago and he is still an active member of the company today. Harman's first product, an FM tuner with just two knobs, was launched in 1953. This was briskly followed a year later by the world's first Hi-Fi receiver (amplifier and tuner combined) – the Harman Kardon Festival D1000. This then led to the introduction of the world's first stereo receiver in 1958, the Festival TA230.

Harman Kardon's reputation for innovation has kept pace with the increasing speed of technological change. For example, in 1999 Harman Kardon's SoundSticks became the first branded computer speakers to win design awards. Today they are regarded as a design classic and are still available on the market. Harman Kardon has also been responsible for advances such as ultrawide-bandwidth two-channel systems, powerful 7.1-channel systems and multi-room solutions.

Throughout its long career in Hi-Fi and audio visual (AV) technology, Harman Kardon has always been at the forefront of technological innovation, with the emphasis on making better sound more accessible to a wider audience.

Recent product launches include Digital Lounge – Harman Kardon's solution to the complicated and often confusing world spawned by the arrival of the now ubiquitous 'HD Ready' generation of products. It offers an integrated partnership of enveloping surround sound and clear vision, with no compromises in quality or looks. Indeed, the high-gloss black finish gives a visual taste of what's to come when the system is activated. Despite incorporating the fruits of all of Harman Kardon's years of audio and AV technological innovation (with every conceivable gizmo and format), Digital Lounge remains easy to use – even for those taking their first steps in their digital lifestyle.

Harman Kardon's range of AV receivers has evolved out of a long line of class-leading products. Elegant, understated fascia design conceals a powerhouse of multi-channel amplification for one or more rooms, delivering high quality stereo and surround-sound at the press of a button. The receivers are supported by some of the most technically advanced DVD players, capable of playback of almost any silver disc format.

The iPod has given rise to a plethora of add-ons and accessories and Harman Kardon was among the first to recognise the potential of this format. Many car manufacturers, including BMW, Mercedes, Range Rover and Saab, have also embraced this technology and chosen to build Harman Kardon technology into their vehicles. Now Drive + Play adds iPod ease-of-use to in-car entertainment, making it possible to play an iPod in the car using Harman Kardon controls which mirror those of an iPod. In 2005, Drive + Play was named as the best car integration product for the iPod and digital music markets by PlaylistMag.com. In addition, in the same year, it was also awarded Playlist's Plays of the Year award for best automotive integration system for iPods and other digital music players.

Also designed with the iPod in mind, this time for home use, The Bridge iPod docking station integrates with home entertainment systems using a single connection. It provides navigation and control of an iPod player with The Bridge-Ready Harman Kardon receiver's remote control, allowing any track, video or still image stored on the iPod player to be played through the connected home entertainment system.

Harmon Kardon still works on Dr Sidney Harman's founding principle: making music the best it can be.

Hotel Chocolat
Quality cocoa, dipped in boutique luxury

086

Armed with passion and enthusiasm, Hotel Chocolat has embarked on a journey to re-set the stakes of the chocolate market in terms of quality, variety and inspiration.

The story began some 14 years ago, when co-founders Angus Thirlwell and Peter Harris made it a personal quest to improve the calibre of the nation's chocolate; initially by way of a compact catalogue selection. This exclusivity led to a cult following that increased demand and spawned an award-winning website. After the launch of www.hotelchocolat.co.uk, brand awareness spread and it wasn't long before Hotel Chocolat took up residence on the high street.

Since 2004, Hotel Chocolat has opened 22 stores across the UK; the look and feel of each meticulously planned to provide a multi-sensory experience. Fundamental to all is an uncluttered, sophisticated feel that, complete with polished stone floors and natural wood interiors, is reminiscent of a boutique-style hotel. Part of the brand's aspirational ethos is to retain some of the sense of exclusivity that initially attracted customers, while preserving an element of enchantment, commonly associated with traditional chocolate shops.

Thanks to its team of in-house specialists, who source and use only bona fide ingredients, Hotel Chocolat has established a reputation for authenticity. This emphasis on quality is strengthened through its own West Indian cocoa plantation, the Rabot Estate, in St Lucia. Purchased in 2005, the 130 acres of prime cocoa growing land, that make up the Rabot Estate,

have been restored to their full former 'working glory', and provide the source of Hotel Chocolat's single estate, single origin, 'Purist Range'.

In St Lucia, Hotel Chocolat was able to put into practice the expertise and knowledge accrued through its links with cocoa growing communities in Ghana, where for several years now it has aided the regeneration of an aged cocoa crop through a seedling development programme. The idea behind both the St Lucian and Ghanaian projects (collectively known as 'Engaged Ethics') is to work with farmers and producers to improve the quality of the cocoa (and ultimately the chocolate made from the cocoa) while sustaining the direct benefits to the communities involved.

Hotel Chocolat has two significant brand extensions: the Tasting Clubs, which engage and invite chocolate lovers to be involved in the creative processes that make up its products; and Hotel Chocolat Corporate, which offers businesses luxury gift solutions for staff and customers.

The brand name implies a chocolate sanctuary, a 'sense of place' where luxury is implicit but there remains an element of mystery and intrigue. The

future of Hotel Chocolat is very much about 'raising the bar' in terms of chocolate quality; it's what has always been, and still is, at the heart of the brand. This goal is motivated and aided by an innovative approach to growing and manufacturing its own products; which are then distributed through a variety of channels to a growing consumer base – both in the UK and globally.

Hotel Chocolat has accrued an array of awards since its inception, from Emerging Retailer of the Year, in the annual Retail Week awards, to Business of the Year at the Cambridge Business Awards. Each accolade reflects the passion, enthusiasm and continued commitment that the brand has to making authentic, quality chocolate – available to everyone.

ICA
Creativity, exploration, discovery

088

As home to some of the best new arts and culture, both nationally and internationally, the Institute of Contemporary Arts (ICA) plays a vital role in determining artistic truths by posing the questions: who are we and how do we live?

Since its inception in 1947 the ICA has established a reputation as one of the world's most innovative and historically influential contemporary art institutions. Originally conceived as a 'laboratory' or 'playground' for contemporary arts by forward thinking artists, philosophers and designers, the ICA's founding principle was 'to stimulate discussion, vitality and daring experiment; providing an alternative to run-of-the-mill museums or bleak exhibition galleries'.

Over the past 60 years the institution has remained true to these ideals, continuing to work across the broadest possible range of artistic and intellectual fields to encourage wider, often unorthodox, understanding of art and culture. Whether through presentation of a current trend or a new idea, individual or movement, the ICA has consistently been at the forefront of cultural exploration.

Importantly, the ICA has been instrumental in the development of significant artistic, philosophical and theoretical movements through abstract expressionism, pop art, post-modernism and debates on race, gender and identity. This prescient thinking extends across its entire programme; through theatre, gigs and club nights, cinema,

exhibitions, digital media, talks and education, as well as through the ICA films, film distribution wing, and the London Consortium PhD programme.

Legendary club nights, Blacktronica and Batmacumba were born at the ICA and more recently the much heralded grime and dubstep night, Dirty Canvas, has taken up residence. Groundbreaking films such as In this World, Kandahar, Osama, and Turtles Can Fly have all lent credence to the reputation of the ICA as one of the first venues to screen significant social and political works from the Middle East. ICA offsite projects have included the infamous Intruders at the Palace musical benefit gig in 1988 featuring David Bowie, amongst many others. Then, in 2004, The Pet Shop Boys present Battleship Potemkin live event in Trafalgar Square was one of the most ambitious projects ever staged in that arena, drawing a crowd of more than 35,000.

The ICA's 60th anniversary is marked in 2007/08 and as the institution celebrates its past it also considers its future, by continuing to challenge traditional notions and boundaries of art forms. Special events to mark the occasion have included: All Tomorrow's Pictures, a photography project in collaboration with Sony Ericsson, where 60 leading contemporary figures across a broad artistic and cultural landscape presented (as both a book and an exhibition) their vision of tomorrow; a gala auction and stellar rendition of regular cult evening, Pecha Kucha, hosted by ICA chairman, Alan Yentob; the first ever iTunes festival, showcasing 31 nights of live music throughout July – from the legendary Paul McCartney to the likes of Amy Winehouse, Mika, Groove Armada and Kasabian; and Beck's Fusions, a stand-out series of events in collaboration with Beck's that culminated in a special public performance live in Trafalgar

Square from The Chemical Brothers, United Visual Artists and special guests.

Through working with artists, curators, musicians, directors and thinkers who share a desire to investigate issues relevant to the wider concerns of today's world, the ICA has created a community of cultural exploration that remains at the forefront of contemporary arts activity. Luminaries such as T S Eliot, Stravinsky, Elizabeth Lutyens, Ronnie Scott, Jackson Pollock, Cartier-Bresson, Keith Haring and Vivienne Westwood (to name but a few) have all played a part in shaping the community of cultural exploration and creativity that defines the ICA and that has kept it at the forefront of vital contemporary activity.

innocent
innocent by name,
innocent by nature

Who says that you can't be successful, do some good and have fun along the way? All it takes is one great idea.

In 1998 three friends came up with just that; the idea of crushing fruit into a small bottle to sell. That summer, armed with £500 worth of fruit, Richard Reed, Adam Balon and Jon Wright set up a stall at a music festival in London, with a sign asking punters if they should give up their jobs to make smoothies instead. The answer – a resounding yes – prompted them to return to work the following day, and resign.

Since these auspicious beginnings innocent has grown rapidly: from three people in a bedroom to over 200 people in eight offices across Europe. Currently the number one smoothie brand in the UK, with a market share of 68 per cent (Source: IRI Infoscan epos sales 2007, w/e 26th April 2007) and an estimated turnover of £100 million in 2007, over 12,000 retailers in the UK, Ireland, France, Denmark, Sweden, Germany, Holland and Belgium now stock innocent drinks.

The focus, at innocent, has always been to make drinks that taste good, and do good – simple given that the ingredients are 100 per cent natural. Recipe development and product innovation are brand priorities. New recipes are continually introduced throughout the year, using new ingredients. This kind of innovation has gained accolades for the brand such as 'Best UK Soft Drink', for four years running, at the Quality Food & Drink Awards – the Oscars of the food world.

innocent launched its kids' smoothies in March 2005, and now has four recipes in outlets across the UK. Furthermore,

since September 2006, 550 schools have started stocking innocent kids' smoothies at a subsidised price, giving more children access to more fruit.

But being natural isn't just about the drinks. At innocent there is an emphasis on making communication – whether internally or with consumers – as down-to-earth as possible. While the 'bananaphone' may sound like a gimmick, there's always a real person at the other end. This personal courtesy extends to staff, as shown by the regular 'start-the-week' staff meeting, held every Monday morning. Meanwhile, new employees are welcomed into the company with flowers and a plethora of lunch-mates, to help them settle into Fruit Towers, innocent's London head quarters.

Sustainability is big business at innocent: whether in terms of sourcing ethical fruit suppliers, declaring its carbon footprint or running offices on green energy; every stage of production is monitored for its environmental impact. It also gives 10 per cent of all profits annually to the innocent foundation – a charity that works with non-government organisations (NGOs) in the countries where its fruit is sourced.

innocent believes that 'doing good' can be fun. This year it held the 'innocent village fete' in Regent's Park with profits going to three charity partners. Activities at the fete included welly-wanging, dog agility trials and ferret racing.

Most of innocent's market is currently in the UK, but this will soon change. Setting its sights firmly on Europe, innocent plans to become the continent's favourite little juice company over the next five to 10 years. Their mums must be proud.

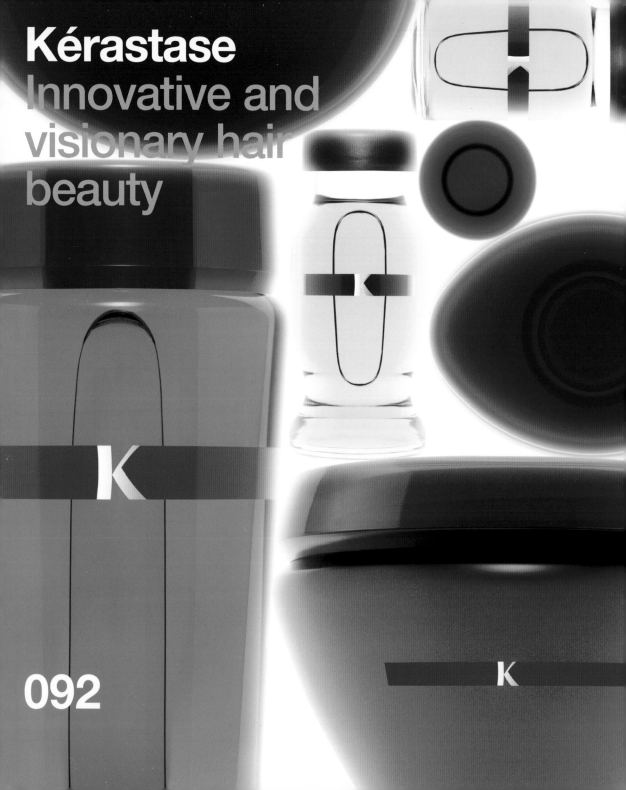

Kérastase
Innovative and visionary hair beauty

092

Kérastase is a pioneer in creating luxury, technically advanced salon haircare products. The brand has innovation at its heart and is much loved for its uncompromising vision.

Kérastase has developed something of a cult following among professional hair stylists, celebrities and leading beauty journalists. Its impeccable credentials have resulted in extensive industry recognition through an array of beauty awards, most recently including four products being recognised in the InStyle awards 2007. In addition, Ciment Thermique was nominated as 'Best New Professional Haircare Product – Prestige' at the Cosmetics Executive Women awards as well as being recognised at the Grazia Hair Awards 2007.

Kérastase has a strong heritage, first making its mark in the 1960s by launching revolutionary in-salon products to cleanse and purify the scalp, forging strong connections with some of the best salons. This relationship has been maintained ever since, working with salons to create the ultimate in luxurious haircare experiences and working with hairdressers to develop innovative products and services.

Kérastase's first professional homecare products were introduced in the 1970s, as women began to wash their hair at home and hairstyle trends became more extravagant. This period saw groundbreaking launches and the creation of new product categories in haircare.

The brand has been continually aware of the changing needs of its customers and has continued to create innovative products. During the 1980s this included the launch of the first complete collection for dry hair and the first sun haircare containing UV filters. In the 1990s, Kérastase personalised its range further with hair masques for fine or thick hair and introduced ingredients such as ceramides and Vita-Ciment®.

In recent years, Kérastase has been working with salons around the UK to develop a new type of in-salon experience – the Kérastase Ritual, where pampering is blended with a strong prescriptive experience. The brand also adopted revolutionary semantics to describe the salon environment and experience: the hair spa area, instead of the basin area, the hair bath instead of the shampoo, or the Rituals instead of the in-salon treatments are all concepts and names that contributed to elevating the consumer experience and establishing the brand's luxury positioning.

Over the past 10 years, Kérastase has been a leading force in promoting the need for an individual haircare 'prescription' for every single client in the salon; a concept today adopted as a norm by almost every salon around the UK. In addition, through new exclusive services such as Kérathermie, an in-salon service using the strength of heat to repair the hair shaft deep down, or more recently the introduction of Le Diagnostic Avancé, a diagnostic protocol for scalp and hair. Using a high-definition camera, Kérastase has taken the salon industry to a new level.

In 2003, Kérastase launched Masque Age Recharge, the very first anti-ageing masque for mature hair; an immediate success, women of all ages quickly became addicted to this nourishing and revitalising hair masque. In 2007, Kérastase complemented the Age Recharge range with a dedicated hair bath (shampoo) and leave-in nourishing and rejuvenating scalp treatment, Lipo-Recharge, creating the first lipo-replenishing, anti-ageing intervention for the scalp and hair.

Kérastase also launched Ciment Thermique in 2007, a heat-activated fortifying milk for weakened hair. This product became an instant beauty must-have, cherished by women looking to not only style their hair more quickly, but also repair it at the same time. Ciment Thermique was undeniably the brand's most successful launch in the past 20 years.

With prescriptive products of unrivalled performance, innovative services and stunning advertising and in-store campaigns, Kérastase continues to be the leading professional luxury haircare brand in the world, a symbol of timeless elegance and hair beauty.

London College
of Fashion
Fashioning
the Future

094

London College of Fashion has been putting would-be designers, tailors and beauty specialists through their sartorial steps ever since 1906.

Situated at the heart of one of the world's cultural capitals, the College draws inspiration from its vibrant surroundings; having identified from the outset the skills needed to succeed in fashion.

During the 1930s – and throughout the ensuing war years – it became apparent that the fledgling 'ready-to-wear' market was beginning to change the direction of the industry. London College of Fashion (LCF) was one of the first educational institutions to recognise this emerging trend and took a pioneering stance, adapting its training accordingly. This radical approach to design education is as prevalent to the brand's ethos today as it was back then.

London College of Fashion is the only UK college to specialise in fashion education, research and consultancy – providing a unique opportunity to study at all levels. From Access and First Diploma through to Postgraduate Certificate and PhD, its expansive remit offers courses from fashion design and technology, management and marketing to communication, promotion and image creation. Its aim: to reflect the breadth of opportunity available in such a creative industry.

Located at the epi-centre of London's garment district – Bond Street, Savile Row, Soho and Great Portland Street – the College offers a dynamic environment in which to study fashion. Its philosophy is to offer creative development alongside a strong vocational slant. The continued expertise of experienced industry professionals (many tutors combining teaching with successful fashion careers) ensures that students are kept up-to-date with the changing demands and opportunities within the industry.

Research at LCF thrives within the College's unique specialist environment and is supported and resourced by dedicated facilities such as its world-class Library and Archive. Research activity within the fashion media and cultural field encompasses curation and exhibition of fashion and fashion photography at international venues, contributions to the global fashion press, editorships of major research and trade journals, and well established links with museums such as the V&A.

Through publicising achievements and success, London College of Fashion aims to ensure that it is the first port of call for anyone looking for design graduates. The brand already has a strong international reputation through its support of overseas projects and recruitment; further enhanced by the ongoing development of research and postgraduate opportunities forging strong links both locally and globally. The College's collaborations with some of fashion's leading innovators looks to challenge convention, generate new ideas and mentor exceptional talent, in ways that enrich the cultural economy.

In the academic year of 2006/07, London College of Fashion celebrated its centenary. Its emphasis on professionalism and innovation during the course of a century has kept it at the forefront of fashion education, collecting influential friends along the way, valued ex-students and industry allies who continue to offer resources and vital tools that keep students in touch with the business world.

London College of Fashion's commitment to nurturing new talent is demonstrated through its brand initiatives. For example, the Centre for Fashion Enterprise – a business development programme working with early stage fashion companies in London – supports talent by helping new starters to develop and build a successful fashion company. Another, the Fashion Business Resource Studio – a one-stop-shop for sharing London College of Fashion's creative, business and technical expertise with fashion and lifestyle industries – provides a mutually supportive culture dedicated to improving the integration of emerging talent, technical expertise, new knowledge and entrepreneurial advice.

Fashion is not simply about styling; it affects key areas such as politics, economics and social futures through issues such as body image and health, as well as ethical and sustainable fashion. Over the years the College, while retaining its educational integrity, has evolved into a place more aware of and open to the dynamic forces defining a global and modern fashion industry.

Photography by Rob Phillips Fashion by Michela Carraro (main image), Shahrin Baharudin (bottom left), Cecilia Mary Robson (bottom right).

Maglite®
Engineered for Brilliance™

maglite.com

CoolBrands 2007/08

Before 1979 the flashlight was regarded as unreliable, a disposable commodity that required regular replacing. The Maglite® design – years in perfecting – revolutionised the portable lighting industry from the moment it appeared.

Maglite®'s creator, Tony Maglica, was born in New York but spent his formative years in Europe, where he received his technical training. He returned to the US in 1950 and with an initial investment of just US$125 put his well-honed skills as an experimental machinist to the test in the inauspicious surroundings of a Los Angeles garage workshop. Despite these somewhat modest beginnings, Maglica soon built up a reputation for combining innovative manufacturing techniques with quality and efficiency. These skills fused with his entrepreneurial spirit in the 1970s when Tony spotted a gap in the market for a niche product – a superior flashlight.

The Maglite® flashlight was launched in 1979, originally targeted at professionals – the likes of firefighters and emergency workers – whose lives (and those of others) often depended on the reliability of their equipment. It wasn't long before these national 'heros' started to insist on using only Maglite®, a trend quickly emulated by general consumers.

In 1982 the Mag Charger® was launched, as the most powerful rechargeable flashlight of its size on the market. By 1984 the company (Mag Instrument, Inc.) had introduced the Mini Maglite® AA flashlight. At less than six inches long

and weighing fewer than 60 grams, it was astonishingly bright compared to other flashlights of similar dimensions. With its aesthetic appeal, unsurpassed functionality and high quality production, it became an instant success. Next, in 1988, came the Solitaire®, a one-cell AAA flashlight with the same rugged aluminum construction, focusing beam and extreme brightness for its size, and yet small enough to carry on a keychain.

All Maglite® flashlights are made from anodised, precision-machined aircraft aluminium and are shock and water-resistant. Consistent product quality and durability have won Maglite® iconic status within American manufacturing and today its range of flashlights are exported to and sold in more than 85 countries worldwide.

Maglica still has a passion for the technical excellence of his products. He runs the company with a hands-on approach, personally overseeing and

executing all product research and development and instilling the core brand philosophy of consistent quality coupled with outstanding service – every step of the way.

One of the elements that makes Maglite® stand out in the current industrial climate – where availability of cheap overseas labour is plentiful – is the brand's refusal to outsource its manufacturing overseas. Mag Instrument's commitment to US based manufacturing can be witnessed in all aspects of the company: design, production, manufacture and staffing. To 'outsource' the manufacture of its flashlights would go against the founding principles.

Each Mag Instrument flashlight is a culmination of more than 25 years research and continuous state-of-the-art refinement in every precision feature. Over the years Maglite® flashlights have accrued elite status within the industry, picking up a cupboard full of design awards and accolades along the way including a recent iF product design award for the Maglite® LED flashlight.

Marshall
Power
Performance
Passion

098

marshallamps.com

CoolBrands 2007/08

More than three generations of musicians have come to rely on the unique sound and quality of Marshall amplifiers, the scripted logo appearing on stage behind numerous top performers, past and present.

Assisted by the exposure of legendary bands such as The Who, Cream and the late Jimi Hendrix, Marshall Amplification achieved worldwide recognition at an early age; the secret of the brand's success being due to its eponymous founder Jim Marshall and his ability to listen.

Beginning his career in music as a singer, Jim later became a drummer and drum teacher before moving into retail in the early 1960s. It soon became apparent that his stock of purely drums and associated equipment needed to be expanded and, guided by his natural entrepreneurial skills, Jim also began to sell guitars and amplifiers.

These same skills were displayed when Jim realised that the guitarists visiting his shop were looking for a more unique sound not offered by any current product and, in response, he began to build his own amplifier. By 1962 the first Marshall amplifier had been produced to great acclaim, and, as the music scene exploded, the brand's growth also continued, with many leading guitarists of the day choosing Marshall amplifiers and cabinets.

It was at this time that Jim created the first 'full stack', where an amplifier head is placed on top of two speaker cabinets, each cabinet holding four 12 inch speakers. The innovation was a direct

response from Jim to the call for more power from guitarists and this established the brand's credentials as the definitive manufacturer of powerful amplifiers.

A move to new premises in Bletchley in 1966 facilitated real expansion and as the next generation of bands such as Deep Purple, Free and Led Zeppelin achieved worldwide success, so too did Marshall Amplification – heralding another move to even larger premises. By 1984 – the year Marshall won the prestigious Queen's Award for Export Achievement – even this site had been outgrown and the factory next door was acquired. Soon after, the company was to win its second Queen's Award.

Marshall Amplification now exports to over 65 countries and has become a name synonymous with quality and craftsmanship. Constant investment in new manufacturing processes, combined with the latest computer-controlled machinery and experienced personnel, ensures the brand's continued success.

Conventional marketing in the major guitarist magazines helps to promote Marshall products. In addition, the company has a presence at all the major UK trade shows. The company also produces a product catalogue each year along with a publication called Marshall Law (now in its tenth year), which features articles about prominent artists who use Marshall equipment. As a brand known for its association with some of the greatest musicians, Marshall is also heavily involved in the UK's festival scene, sponsoring stages and supporting artists. At the Download festival for example, each year Marshall supplies a 'warm-up' tent where artists can jam using Marshall amplifiers before they appear on stage.

The Marshall website offers comprehensive information on virtually every product and offers a host of

resources including artist quotes, artist interviews, a gig guide, online lessons and downloads. A recent addition to the site is the 'Marshall Theatre', a vehicle for streaming video footage of both products and artists.

The brand also collaborates with other leading names such as O2 – which featured a Marshall amplifier in its recent Millennium Dome campaign – and Pure, resulting in the manufacture of a DAB radio which reflects the identity of a Marshall amplifier.

However, the most effective advertisement for Marshall products remains the amplifiers and cabinets themselves which appear on stages worldwide. Thanks to his uncompromising vision, Jim Marshall has created a product synonymous with power, quality and craftsmanship that continues to inspire musicians of every style, every age and every ability.

Mexico
A colourful fusion of old and new

visitmexico.com

CoolBrands 2007/08

Steeped in history and culture, Mexico is where the ancient and modern worlds harmoniously come together – a unique land that values both its present and its past.

Located in the northern region of the American continent, Mexico – its name originating from the traditional Nahuatl language of the Aztecs – sits between the Pacific Ocean and the Gulf of Mexico, bordered by the US in the north and Guatemala and Belize in the south. Mexico extends over a vast area of some 1,964,375 sq km, which is divided into six distinctive tourist regions: Northern Mexico; Central Mexico; Southern Mexico; The Yucatan Peninsula; the Pacific Coast; and the Baja California Peninsula – each with their own climate, customs and indigenous terrain. This ranges from desert to rugged mountain ranges and white sand beaches to forests.

Mexico, the brand, was created four years ago, a co-venture between the then CEO of the Mexico Tourism Board and one of the country's leading graphic designers. The unified vision was to convey the vastness and cultural diversity of the Mexican identity internationally, under just one banner: Mexico. The essence of the brand is built around the notion of expressing the original nature of the Mexican people (both past and present), a unique fusion of ancient and modern day.

The resulting product, a tourism office, is responsible for the promotion of all aspects of Mexican tourism via a range of marketing activities. In the UK, in addition to the more conventional forms of advertising such as the media (print and TV), billboards, buses and cabs the brand also operates through less traditional channels; film festivals, gallery openings, and perhaps most importantly in terms of international recognition, museum exhibitions. Recent high-profile exhibitions that have highlighted the brand include 'The Aztecs' at the Royal Academy of Arts, 'Frida Kahlo' at Tate Modern, and Tina Modotti and Edward Weston's exhibition at the Barbican Centre. Established artists are also seen to look to Mexican culture for ideas and inspiration as illustrated by Damian Hirst's 'Diamond School', a piece heavily influenced by Mexico.

But the brand is about much more than promoting tourism and development alone, encompassing all aspects of the Mexican identity and its products such as trade, foreign investment and cultural interchange.

The brand's meaning is clearly defined by its logo, with the image and essence implicit within the name of the nation itself. Therefore, no other promotional visual aides or additions are deemed necessary to convey its message.

Every letter of the brand logo symbolises a different product or essence, represented by a relevant colour: M, for ancient civilisation; E, for a nation born from two worlds; X, the crossroads of the two cultures melted into one; I, the modernity of the nation, based in the country's roots; C, its rich natural resources, vitality and varied bio-diversity; and O, the all encompassing seas, skies and natural beauty.

Since its inception the brand has accrued various international awards, but it remains the country itself with its unique complex heritage, natural beauty and cultural diversity that is truly deserving of global recognition.

Nokia
Iconic,
innovative,
stylish

102

NOKIA

Since launching the first hand-held mobile phone in 1987, Nokia has pushed the boundaries of design and technology to become a leader in mobile communications.

Nokia uses innovative technology to create cutting-edge and easy-to-use products that respond to the changing needs of its customers – devices with cameras, MP3 players, radios, mobile email, internet connectivity and more. Mobile phones are a huge part of people's lives, and Nokia offers products that connect people to their passions, and to the people that matter to them.

Nokia's devices were the first to feature text messaging, integrated cameras and MP3 players, and to access internet-based information services. Today, Nokia continues to innovate with its Nseries range of high performance multimedia computers, which includes the Nokia N95 – the first device with in-built GPS – and its Eseries devices that offer optimised solutions to business users. In 2006 Nokia sold more than 140 million camera phones and over 70 million devices with music capabilities, making it the world's largest manufacturer of cameras and digital music players.

In addition, Nokia continues to redefine the mobile gaming experience with its next generation gaming platform; the N-Gage brand is evolving from a device offering games and services to a comprehensive, interactive mobile gaming experience available on Nokia Nseries and Series 60 devices.

Design remains a fundamental building block of the Nokia brand, with handsets such as the Nokia 8800 becoming

design classics. The first to introduce colour and changeable covers, Nokia's reputation for iconic design continues with its catwalk inspired Fashion Collections and 2007's Nokia 6300 handset, which combines a contemporary edge with classic elegance.

Nokia was one of the first technology brands to work with the fashion industry, sponsoring London Fashion Week from 1999 to 2004 and working with leading designers including Kenzo, Donatella Versace, Cath Kidston and Giambattista Valli. Nokia is also sponsor of the Glamour Women of the Year Awards and has sponsored the Clothes Show Live for the last two years.

Nokia is also involved in a range of innovative music-led projects; in 2006, www.MusicRecommenders.com launched – a unique download service enabling music fans to explore new music personally recommended by 40 of the world's most influential independent record stores. Users can browse and buy tracks, getting an insight into new music through city music guides and artist interviews; music legend David Bowie is a regular contributor of exclusive features, podcasts, commentary and recommendations.

In 2006, Nokia also launched a mobile ticketing service, www.ticketrush.co.uk – a free service giving registered users the chance to buy tickets before the general

public. It also updates them by text message of any last minute tickets for sold-out gigs.

Nokia supports grassroots music. Its Rock Up & Play initiative, now in its third year, provides people with the opportunity to simply 'rock up and play' at Nokia hosted gigs. Rock Up & Play at the Carling Weekend Festivals included Q&A sessions, giving festival-goers the chance to interact with their favourite bands.

As a sponsor of ITV's The X-Factor for the last three years, Nokia has taken it beyond the TV screen and into the streets of the UK, giving fans across the UK the chance to win tickets to see The X-Factor finalists perform live.

Through all its activities, Nokia's aim is to enrich people's lives by creating products and experiences that help them live their lives to the full.

Oakley
High Definition Optics®

It started with a single idea. Jim Jannard, a self-confessed mad scientist, looked at a product and saw an opportunity.

Using his first invention, 'Unobtainium' – a synthetic, sticky-feeling plastic, that unlike other grip materials improved when wet – he developed a motocross handgrip like no other.

The year was 1975. It was the beginning of Oakley Inc, a technology company that would become devoted to innovation in the sports industry.

Jannard started the company with an initial investment of US$300 and named it after his dog. Using the patented Unobtainium throughout a performance eyewear range, and thanks to the breakthrough Oakley O-Frame goggles, he went on to build the brand in motocross, BMX and snowboarding.

Reinventing the concept of eyewear was only the first step. Oakley's desire to invent and evolve 'stuff' for the core sports loved by the Oakley team led it into high-performance watches, apparel, footwear and accessories. This passion meant that during the 1980s, when the worlds of snowboarding and BMX filtered into the street fashion market, Oakley could evolve organically into a global lifestyle brand.

Oakley has since established itself as the undisputed leader in sports performance eyewear and apparel, holding a unique position within 'core' sports – skate, wake, snowboard, ski, BMX, MTB, surf – and traditional sports, including golf, rowing, sailing, cricket, cycling, triathlon and athletics. No other brand can claim to be as authentic in both. The diversity

of the Oakley product mix is reflected in a pro-athlete team that consists of Tour de France legend Lance Armstrong, rising BMX star Shanaze Reade, pro golfer Ian Poulter, British snowboard champion Vicci Miller (viccislife.co.uk), skateboarder Ben Grove (benslife.co.uk) and surfer Oli Adams (olislife.co.uk).

Oakley is not a brand that stands still. It invents and reinvents products, then engineers the machinery to build and refine them. There is no blueprint to follow; Oakley invented that too. It is its patented optical innovations that really set it apart from the rest. One such innovation, defined as Oakley High Definition Optics (HDO®), represents the brand's superior lens offer. HDO® promises razor sharp lens clarity, zero distortion, 100 per cent UV filtering and unrivaled impact protection.

Oakley continues to differentiate itself from traditional action sports brands by challenging consumer perceptions. Its current mission is to challenge the misconception that the Oakley brand is only applicable to men and extreme sports. The Oakley Women's brand is growing fast, following the launch of three female-specific lifestyle frames in 2006. The message behind the range is that fashion-conscious, active women can now have style and performance. A contemporary lifestyle and beach apparel line completes the Oakley Women's offering.

Another key initiative for 2007 and beyond is the Oakley Eye-Q consumer education programme. Designed to raise awareness of the risks of UV-related eye damage and poor quality sunglasses, the campaign will be launched by England cricketer Kevin Pietersen and Radio 1 health expert Dr Mark Hamilton. Various consumer research projects and educational events are planned.

In the UK Oakley will continue to place British athletes at the centre of its advertising. In 2007, the 'Square O' eyewear campaign will be executed across outdoor, print and retail platforms, whilst the 'O-Life' apparel campaign will be communicated through a unique athlete-led microsite. In addition, it will develop its wider lifestyle links with the continued sponsorship of 'Oakley Unsigned' and 'Clash Club' – a national search for new music talent and a monthly live music gig that has already seen The Fratellis and The Kooks grace the stage. Furthermore, in celebration of the Tour de France coming to London, Oakley will launch Radar, a new sports performance piece, and showcase its cycling heritage through a unique brand museum at the Getty Images Gallery.

Peroni Nastro Azzurro
Italian Style In A Bottle

The Italians have a saying for always looking and acting your best: 'La bella figura' – the beautiful figure. This ethos lies at the heart of Peroni Nastro Azzurro, guiding how it is poured, drunk and displayed… impressions count.

Launched in Italy in the 1960s as an international premium brand, Peroni Nastro Azzurro quickly gained notoriety alongside other timeless, iconic and aspirational style leaders such as Gucci, Ferrari, Prada and Vespa.

Inspired by Peroni's roots, the current advertising campaign uses Fellini's seminal 1960's film La Dolce Vita to encapsulate the brand as the essence of Italian style. The campaign re-shot scenes from Fellini's masterpiece including the one immortalised by Anita Ekberg in Rome's Trevi fountain – the first time that permission had been granted to film in the fountain since the original film was made.

As part of this work, world famous war photographer Tom Stoddart was commissioned for the brand's press and outdoor campaign. The result: a collection of iconic images that convey the essence of 1960s style and the birth of Peroni Nastro Azzurro, displayed on premium outdoor sites across London, Manchester, Liverpool, Glasgow and Edinburgh as well as in style press titles such as Vogue, GQ, Vanity Fair and Wallpaper*.

Following the success of its La Dolce Vita commercial, Peroni Nastro Azzurro has immersed itself in the world of film

through partnerships with arthouse cinemas across London. Complimentary bottles of Peroni are served by models in 1960s usherette attire and retro filmic posters advertise the Peroni re-make, itself screened prior to the main feature and projected within the cinema's foyer.

The past year has also seen the La Dolce Vita advertising successfully take to the streets of London via 'Cinema Peroni' – a customised camper van with a high powered projector and sound system, projecting the advert onto prominent buildings in high footfall areas such as Soho, Kings Road, Leicester Square and Regent Street. To add further style to the event, velvet seats were positioned on pavements, encouraging the public to sit back and enjoy the film with fresh popcorn handed out by Peroni usherettes.

This year, Peroni Nastro Azzurro became the first beer to officially partner with London Fashion Week. In the past Peroni has appeared at the week-long event, requested by individual designers for private parties, and this year was no different with the brand featuring at Christopher Kane, Erdem, Gharani Strok, Ben de Lisi and Kenzo VIP events. In addition, Peroni continues to support menswear designers Man and Rushmoor – a brand whose Spring/Summer 2007 menswear fashion shows were hosted by Peroni in Italy in September 2006.

Peroni Nastro Azzurro has also collaborated with the world's leading style bible, Vogue Italia, to create a photographic retrospective which showcases their contribution to 50 Years of Italian Style. The exhibition takes place during September's London Fashion Week at the Royal Academy of Arts.

Today, Peroni Nastro Azzurro has become highly representative of classic Italian style and culture. By using only

the finest quality and variety of spring barley, maize, malts and hops and by following a meticulous production process a distinctive crisp and refreshing taste is delivered, perfect for pairing with speciality food dishes. From July 2007, internationally renowned Italian chef Giorgio Locatelli will be starring in Peroni branded press advertising and creating bespoke food recipes that are ideal to serve with a bottle of Peroni.

Positioned as 'Italian style in a bottle', from presentation to pouring the Peroni brand has struck a chord with urbanites looking for cosmopolitan class. Peroni Nastro Azzurro. It's not just a beer… it's a fashion statement.

PLAY.COM
Retail revolutionaries

PLAY.COM is a revolutionary retailer offering a vast range of music, film, books, gadgets and electricals. It offers free delivery on everything, which is one reason why its customer service is award-winning.

PLAY.COM started as play247.com over 10 years ago during an age when people were still saying things like: "Have you ever heard of Digital Versatile Discs? They might be the next big thing. Or they may go the way of laser discs." It was during this time that three born and raised Jersey islanders decided they might try to sell them via a mail order catalogue. These new Digital Versatile Disc things (from now on referred to as DVDs) proved to be a success, so they decided to use the internet – also still in its infancy – to sell from. They created a website which created a digital version of their catalogue. This proved to be a major turning point and sales quadrupled overnight.

The site has continued to be a success due to the vision of its founders. They placed emphasis on the content of the site, with information about each of the DVDs being of the highest calibre and well researched. In order to gain customer support above and beyond any of its competitors, they decided to stock every DVD release from 'Railways of Southern Wales' to 'The Matrix' whilst making a website that was fluent, friendly and user friendly. In addition to this, they also realised how important price had become to consumers so aimed to make all prices unbeatable. This foresight has served the islanders well and PLAY.COM

is now a huge presence for online retail in Europe. Its original team of 10 has become a team of over 700.

PLAY.COM now has more than one million products listed on the site and acts as a one-stop shop for a vast range of entertainment needs. From blockbuster DVDs and chart CDs to next generation games consoles and games, as well as high definition LCD TVs and MP3 players, all significantly cheaper than on the high street. Furthermore, PLAY.COM offers the year's bestselling paperbacks to beautiful collectors' books as well as thousands of fun gadgets and gizmos.

As PLAY.COM's range has increased, its policy of not charging for postage and packing has remained the same – it is always completely free on everything. Items that are in stock are usually dispatched within 24 hours and delivered within 1-3 working days. Its customer service through telephone and email aims to ensure that every customer has a stress free buying experience.

The brand has been a consistent award winner, picking up may accolades including: The British Video Association's Retail Success of the Year award every

year since 2004; Number One Wesbite in the Video & Games category in 2004, 2005 and 2006 from Hitwise as well as Number One Website in the Music category from 2004 to 2006; PLAY.COM was also shortlisted at the Bookseller Retail Awards in the Expanding the Retail Market and Direct to Consumer Bookselling Company of the Year categories; also in 2006, it was voted number two in the IMRG-Hitwise Hot Shops List of the top 50 UK e-retailers.

PLAY.COM has played a significant role in revolutionising the way leisure and entertainment products are purchased. As next generation technology and entertainment are developed, PLAY.COM will undoubtedly be at the forefront in delivering it to the consumer.

Main image © Lisa Thornberg

Poggenpohl
Function and
elegance

Poggenpohl kitchens are so modern, so 'of the moment', that it comes as somewhat of a shock to discover that the company dates back to 1892.

Perhaps less surprising is the fact that its founder, Friedemir Poggenpohl, was a German master cabinetmaker with a simple mission 'to improve the kitchen' – an aim that is as apparent in the company's products today as it was over 110 years ago.

Just when you think the kitchen can't possibly be improved upon, or progressed, that is precisely what Poggenpohl does. In 1928, Poggenpohl introduced the Reform Kitchen with its connecting units and integrated storage space.

Then, in 1950, the Form 1000 was introduced. It was the first modern fitted kitchen, as we now know them. Poggenpohl worked closely with appliance manufacturers of the day to integrate its wall and base units with the early versions of must-have labour-saving devices for modern homeowners. Later developments saw the introduction of laminate finishes, colour, under lit wall units, smooth-opening drawers and spring hinges.

In 1970, Poggenpohl unveiled its most radical vision yet; the Experiment 70, featuring a round cooking area, or 'meal preparing unit', 2.4 metres across, in which the user could perform all kitchen tasks at the push of a button from the comfort of a swivel armchair. Monitors and microphones provided communications links to the rest of the house. Experiment 70 never entered production, but it did inspire later

innovations, such as the concept of critical distances and workflow principles, still found at the heart of modern kitchens today.

In 1982 came the +DIMENSION75 kitchen, with revolutionary recessed storage space behind the base units, while 1989 saw the launch of the Form 2400, which, in its choice of colours, surfaces and design accents, was unlike anything the world had seen before. At the dawn of the 21st century came the +ALU2000 aluminium kitchen and the new +PETFOIL eco-friendly laminate, which were followed by the award-winning +SEGMENTO and +INTEGRATION ranges. Sir Terence Conran chose Poggenpohl's +ALU2000 design for his garden at the Chelsea Flower Show in 2004, commenting: "Poggenpohl's design philosophy very much mirrors my own. Their kitchens and accessories combine aesthetics, ergonomics and functionality to beautiful effect."

In 2005, PLUSMODO illustrated how Poggenpohl still dominates the kitchen industry through revolutionary design and product development. The result of a year-long collaboration with world-renowned Spanish furniture designer Jorge Pensi, PLUSMODO meets his desire to create 'a poetic dialogue between display and concealment' by marrying open and closed functional areas.

PLUSMODO features concealed, handle-less drawers embedded into an extra-thick work surface, which appears to float above the base units. Other features include subtly back-lit satin glass and aluminium splash-backs, hanging rails for utensils, timers, a radio and speakers, and above the hob, a concealed extractor. Large, pull-out trays cleverly inserted between the base units and the worktops create additional storage

elements, and can have clear glass inserts added to transform them into display cabinets.

Poggenpohl and Pensi believe that many of today's modern kitchen gadgets, china, glassware, saucepans and utensils, while still functional everyday objects, are themselves works of art and deserve to be seen in all their glory. Lighting has been used to subtly highlight design elements and display areas, while also providing optimal illumination for food preparation areas. Clearly, PLUSMODO has struck a chord, receiving four awards, including the Good Design Award from the Chicago Athenaeum Museum of Architecture and Design, an iF product design award and a Red Dot design award.

Poggenpohl has been at the forefront of kitchen design since the 19th century, ensuring the highest standards of fittings and construction, pioneering the use of new materials and technologies, and continually testing the boundaries of design to improve the kitchen. In the past 18 months, Poggenpohl has increased its showroom network in the UK from 25 to 31, following an 80 per cent increase in unit sales during 2005/06.

Rachel's Organic
It's all here in black and white

It takes a pioneering spirit to make a difference. Rachel's Organic, its heritage steeped in natural farming methods, has done just that – with fate playing a small, but significant helping hand.

Co-founders Gareth and Rachel Rowlands come from a family rooted in organic farming; Rachel's mother was one of the first to sign up to the Soil Association back in 1952. Furthermore, their family dairy farm in Wales was the UK's first certified organic dairy – long before 'organic' became part of the mainstream psyche.

The foundations of the brand were set in winter 1982. Severe snow storms hit, preventing milk tankers from collecting milk produced by the pedigree herd of Guernsey cows. Faced with frozen water supplies, Rachel skimmed off the cream from the daily milk to give back to the cows to drink. To cope with the extra cream that had built up, Rachel resurrected her grandmother's butter churn and began making yogurt. Demand for stock from local shops and hotels soon took off.

Two years later the full potential of the fledgling venture became apparent. Throughout the UK the organic movement was gathering momentum with consumers becoming increasingly concerned with food origins and production. During this transitional time Sainsbury's, who had already started to forge links with organic producers, approached the brand; the rest is history.

By 1998, to reflect the brand's premium credentials, the packaging was changed

to a striking new black and white design that significantly boosted sales and brand awareness. Almost overnight Rachel's Organic became an aspirational brand for 'foodies'.

Rachel's Organic was acquired by leading US organic milk producer, Horizon Organic Dairy in 1999, a company which shared its progressive ethos. The major investment that followed saw Rachel's spearheading the development of a UK market for branded organic milk – once more reinforcing the premium nature of organic dairy products.

New yogurt ranges, branded Welsh butters, deserts and 'Little Rachel's' children's products have now been added to the brand's expanding portfolio, attracting further high profile stockists including IKEA and Eurostar.

One thing has never changed – products are made with organic milk, with no preservatives or artificial sweeteners. Rachel's yogurts combine pasteurised milk, from some of Britain's best-known organic farms, with traditional yogurt and health-promoting live cultures. This focus on quality control has helped the brand to rate consistently highly in taste tests, collecting a cabinet-full of industry awards along the way.

The launch of National Organic Dairy Week in 2006 – extolling the benefits of both organic dairy consumption and

farming practices – underlines the brand's commitment to educating consumers. Rachel's Organic has consistently demonstrated its corporate social responsibility, contributing to charities that include The National Trust and Send a Cow.

Having pioneered the use of black to denote premium quality, the brand found that this was being increasingly imitated, particularly in the food packaging sector. A redesign of the range's packaging was required to give the brand greater differentiation, whilst still reflecting its aspirational, organic credentials. The solution needed to appeal to the growing numbers of more mainstream urban organics followers as well as maintaining the support of its original stylish foodie fans.

In March 2007, Rachel's Organic, unveiled a dramatic new look – dubbed The Rachel's 2007 Collection. The previous black and white design elements had been evolved, whilst introducing a lighter note of patterns, tapping into the current revival of geometric motifs as well as introducing more colour to give clearer distinction between the ranges.

The result has been widely acclaimed, making Rachel's Organic 'must-have fridge candy', reflecting consumer aspirations and values. Rachel's Organic has raised the bar for the next stage of its life.

Rough Guides
The ultimate travel companion

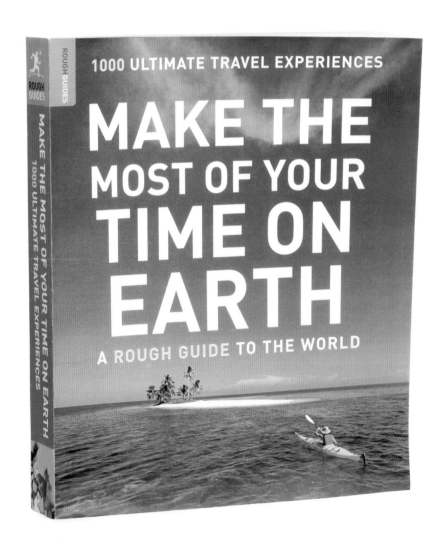

1000 ULTIMATE TRAVEL EXPERIENCES

MAKE THE MOST OF YOUR TIME ON EARTH

A ROUGH GUIDE TO THE WORLD

'In 1981, unable to secure a 'proper job', Rough Guide founder, Mark Ellingham, decided to backpack through Greece. The result: the first Rough Guide.

This saw the start of a trailblazing genre that has encouraged a generation of travellers to visit places that they have never been to.

Despite being penned from the less than scenic surroundings of a housing association flat in South London, the pioneering independent travel guide (which stood out thanks to its quirky, handmade appearance) was an immediate success, encouraging Ellingham and a group of friends to produce 19 further titles over the next five years.

In 1987, Ellingham and a selection of Rough Guide writers bought the series from publisher, Routledge; the group included current travel publisher Martin Dunford – whose Rough Guide credentials dated back to the first guide when he accommodated Ellingham for a short time in Thessaloniki. Ellingham and Dunford continue to run the Rough Guides series, today published by Penguin.

What began as a backpacker's bible has, over the last 25 years, evolved into a brand that offers comprehensive guides, not just on travel but on a wide range of cultural topics as diverse as The Rough Guide to Pregnancy & Birth and the Rough Guide to the Universe. While the original rough-and-ready appearance has been replaced by a glossy cover and full-colour photography, the essence of the brand – producing readable, reliable, well-researched content – remains unchanged. Rough Guides adopts a

journalistic approach that differentiates the brand from its market competitors. Accommodation and restaurant reviews are critical observations as opposed to bland descriptions and the brand demands high standards of both research and writing.

Since its inception Rough Guides has had four major makeovers, with content evolving from the rudimentary publications of 1982 to the detailed handbooks of today. The last significant change was in 2002, when a complete redesign unveiled full-colour introductory sections and two-colour printing throughout. In 2006, the covers also benefited from a re-vamp; the spines of the books are now a uniform colour – a vibrant take on the trademark Rough Guide blue – making the brand easier to identify on the shelf. The distinctive Rough Guide logo of the running man is leaner, located uniformly on the spines and there is a bold orange tab in the top left hand corner of every book.

As technology advances so does the accessibility to destination information and Rough Guides has pioneered modern methods of relaying content. Rough Guides podscrolls, for instance, are a revolutionary format for putting guidebook content onto a colour screen iPod. In February 2007 the brand announced partnerships with leading mobile communications companies, Motorola and Samsung, to carry Rough Guide information on their phones.

In 2007 Rough Guides teamed up with licensee Peter Black to launch Rough Guides branded products, aimed at the outdoor, adventurous and independent traveller which will hit the shelves of Argos, Debenhams and NEXT.

To celebrate Rough Guide's 25th anniversary in 2007, it launched a series limited edition pocket guides featuring 'ultimate travel experiences' charting

unmissable places to visit and things to do, as well as themes such as wonders of the world, wildlife and ethical travel. Rough Guides also launched a guide covering 1,000 must-do experiences from across the globe, entitled 'Make the Most of Your Time on Earth'.

Rough Guides has been at the forefront of an industry led campaign for more responsible travel, teaming up in 2006 with Climate Care to support a carbon offsetting scheme. The Rough Guide to Climate Change was shortlisted for the prestigious Royal Society Prize for Science Books in April 2007 and commended by judges for its presentation of a topical subject in such an accessible way.

Rough Guides has an enviable reputation for telling it how it is, its uncompromising no-nonsense approach winning it both industry and public acclaim. Trading on wit, up-to-date information and an engaging chatty style it does what few other guides have succeeded in doing: demystifies travel and popular culture in an informative and entertaining way.

Rubik's Cube
Forty-three quintillion configurations.
Only one solution.

rubiks.com

CoolBrands 2007/08

In the mid 1970s Erno Rubik, a lecturer in the Department of Interior Design at the Academy of Applied Arts and Crafts in Budapest, set himself a challenge.

He wanted to create a three dimensional object, of a high aesthetic value, which was not only richer in configuration variations and more of a mental challenge than any puzzle in existence, but also one which would continue to be a self-contained whole, all through its manifold transformations. He succeeded and, as it would turn out, had just invented the world's biggest-selling toy.

Rubik and what he then called his 'Magic Cube' caught the imagination of friends and students alike. It also proved popular in the toyshops of Budapest and went on to make its international debut in 1980 at the toy fairs of London, Paris, Nürnberg and New York. In May that year, Rubik's Cube was launched in the US at a Hollywood party hosted by Hungarian actress Zsa Zsa Gabor.

The Cube's success began to rapidly snowball, winning the highest prize for outstanding inventions in Hungary as well as top toy awards in Germany, France, Britain and the US. In 1981 it was entered as an exhibit in the hallowed halls of the New York Museum of Modern Art.

By 1982, the Cube had become a phenomenon. It achieved universal presence and was a household name, even gaining its own entry in the Oxford English Dictionary. Seven Towns Ltd became co-owners and custodians of the brand in the 1980s – a position which the company still holds today.

Brand development then took place, with variants of the original such as the Rubik's Snake, as well as many other puzzles like the two-dimensional Rubik's Magic which have garnered considerable success in their own right.

In 1982 the inaugural World Rubik's Championships were staged in the Cube's physical and spiritual birthplace, Budapest. October 2007, 25 years later, sees the official World Cubing Championship returning, where the competitors will be looking to solve a Rubik's Cube in well under 20 seconds to take the title.

Today, fascination with the Cube continues – seen as 'the' generic name for intriguing puzzles, its images are used under license in TV, film and advertising, on t-shirts, lottery scratch cards, jewellery and in mobile gaming. Internet solutions are offered on around 50,000 sites, giving even the most hopeless of puzzle fans a way to return their Cubes to their natural state.

The most expensive Rubik's Cube was the Masterpiece Cube, produced by Diamond Cutters International in 1995. This actual size, fully-functional cube features 22.5 carats of amethyst,

34 carats of rubies, and 34 carats of emeralds, all set in 18-carat gold, and was valued at approximately 1.5 million US dollars.

Erno Rubik, who still lives in his native Budapest, remains proud of his creation 30 years on. He comments, "Nobody has been able to improve on the basic design, which pleases me as a designer… or on the engineering, which pleases me as an engineer". Yet Rubik's Cube remains a mystery to so many.

S. Pellegrino
Italian by name.
Italian by nature.

118

sanpellegrino.com

CoolBrands 2007/08

The foothills of the Italian Alps provide the source of S. Pellegrino, a mineral water with a composition that has remained the same over hundreds of years.

The town of San Pellegrino, in the Lombardy region of Northern Italy, has long been associated with natural health benefits. In 1839, it became a spa resort, building up a rejuvenating reputation that continues to attract visitors from all parts of the globe today. In 1899, the San Pellegrino Company was founded and began distributing, what has since become one of the world's oldest and most established bottled mineral waters. Over 35,000 bottles were sold during S. Pellegrino's first year of production – 5,500 of those going overseas.

A key part of the enduring appeal of S. Pellegrino lies in its active ingredients: a combination of 14 minerals and natural trace elements. One litre of S. Pellegrino contains 20 per cent of the recommended daily amount of calcium and 16 per cent of the recommended amount of magnesium.

S. Pellegrino is an anti-uric mineral water with a composition that has remained unchanged since its first official analysis took place back in the late 1700s. It emerges from source at a constant temperature of 25-26 degrees, containing a distinct blend of elements – components that also make up the human body. A rare, perfect combination of dissolved minerals and natural CO_2 gives S. Pellegrino its pleasant, refreshing and lightly sparkling taste.

While S. Pellegrino has been an inherent part of Italian lifestyle for over a century,

its appeal extends much further than its country of origin. It now exports to over 110 countries, with 75 per cent of total sales coming from overseas. In 1957 it added Acqua Panna, a still mineral water from the hills of Tuscany, to its portfolio.

Brand promotion of S. Pellegrino seeks to enhance its strong links to the art of choosing, cooking and eating good food. In 2007 – for the first time – it became the leading sponsor of the 'Oscars' of the gastronomy industry. The S. Pellegrino World's 50 Best Restaurants list, which is compiled by a selection of prominent food writers, critics, publishers and commentators. Now in its sixth year it has grown into an internationally influential event, globally recognised as a credible indicator of the best places to eat.

The S. Pellegrino Cooking Cup is an annual regatta held on the waterways of Venice which puts cooking and sailing skills to the test. The brand's involvement reinforces its connection with the Italian way of life by combining three leading Italian passions: food,

classical architecture and sporting prowess. 2006 saw the first British entry in the event's six year history when Tom Aitkens, the youngest ever Michelin starred British chef, climbed aboard to demonstrate his skills – collecting the award for 'Best International Chef' along the way. Angela Hartnett showcased her repertoire in 2007 and won the coveted title again for the UK.

S. Pellegrino has strong brand values rooted in its Italian heritage: tradition, quality and authenticity. These, like its mineral water, continue to stand the test of time.

Saatchi Gallery
Creating an
audience for
new art

120

saatchi-gallery.co.uk

CoolBrands 2007/08

In a world where anyone can be an artist and everybody is a critic, it takes innovation to break boundaries and set standards. The Saatchi Gallery has a reputation for doing both.

By championing the work of young – and largely unseen – artists, as well as displaying rarely exhibited work by established international names, the Saatchi Gallery has built up one of the most stimulating and up-to-date art collections in the world. During the past two decades its pioneering exhibitions have showcased work by over 150 artists and provided a unique springboard for young unknowns to launch their careers – and, as with the likes of Damien Hirst and Jeff Koons, go on to acquire international fame.

When the Saatchi Gallery first opened its doors to the public in 1985, access to contemporary art was regarded by many as the privilege of a specialist few. Collector and founder, Charles Saatchi, believed contemporary art should be available to everyone; that it should become integrated into a nation's culture. By supporting and showing the work of Young British Artists (YBAs), the Saatchi Gallery set a precedent in the art world; fuelling interest in and contributing to the growing popularity of contemporary art. More than 600,000 people visit the Saatchi Gallery each year, with half of all visitors aged between 18 and 34 years-old. In its last two years alone, 1,350 schools have organised student group visits, testament to the brand's accessibility and educational credentials.

In May 2006 the Saatchi Gallery launched its website, which now receives 40 million hits a day on average, making it the world's largest interactive art gallery. Over 50,000 artists, 1,000 commercial galleries, all the world's major museums and art colleges are free to show their work, collections and exhibition highlights. As a result a wave of diverse new works has been made available to a far broader audience and artists, collectors, dealers, students, and all those interested in contemporary art can access visuals and information directly and chat live.

In May 2007 the Saatchi Gallery launched a bespoke website in Mandarin, which allows the Chinese art world to have its own site that functions in the same way as the English speaking site. This created the first interactive art site in Chinese which provides an excellent communications portal between the largely non-English speaking Chinese contemporary art scene and a global audience.

The Saatchi Gallery epitomises passion and vision – a commitment to contemporary art that has helped to establish London as one of the world's leading cultural capitals. As a brand it does not shy away from controversy, choosing to exhibit cutting-edge works by the latest artistic talent, however provocative these are deemed to be. The uncompromising stance has made the Gallery what it is today: a trendsetter – influencing and inspiring both the current, and next, generation of artists and art lovers.

Through its website and dedicated exhibition programme – that focuses on new work by up and coming artists – the brand ensures that it remains fresh and in the public eye, offering its audience the opportunity to experience works that might otherwise only be seen through reproductions.

Collaborations with selective corporate and media sponsors on a number of shows not only benefit the Gallery but also, by association, demonstrate a sponsor's commitment to creativity, innovation and forward-thinking.

So what next? In early 2008 the Saatchi Gallery re-opens in its new central location at the Duke of York HQ right in the heart of fashionable London, on Kings Road, Chelsea. It will be the world's largest contemporary art museum with 50,000 square feet of state-of-the-art gallery space. The Saatchi Gallery plans, through its Corporate Partnerships, to enable free entry to the gallery, and to all temporary exhibitions. It will be the first contemporary art museum to do this.

The inaugural exhibitions will, in keeping with the essence of the brand, highlight exciting new artists from Europe, China and the US.

The Saatchi Gallery will also continue its goal of creating the world's first truly international arts communications portal by creating different language versions of the site in those areas where English is not widely spoken.

Main image © Zhang Xiaogang, 2007 Additional images © Kristin Baker, 2007 (top), © Huma Bhabha, 2007 (bottom)

Samsung
Technology is
the future

122

Samsung Electronics combines technology with innovative design to produce market leading digital TVs, memory chips, mobile phones and TFT-LCDs. It is a global business employing approximately 138,000 people in 56 countries.

For over half a century, Samsung employees have been guided by a corporate philosophy that focuses on superior products and services. This emphasis has, in the last decade, seen Samsung Electronics evolve into one of the world's most influential technology companies.

Five years ago, Samsung pledged to re-position its brand, aligning itself with premium products – a goal it has achieved through launches like the R7/R8 range of LCD TVs, the Ultra range of mobile phones and the J-Series range of home appliances. In May 2007, Samsung launched the Samsung Refrigerator J-Series bringing style, quality and an element of 'cool' to the kitchen.

Enhanced by an aggressive marketing strategy, Samsung's approach to product design has produced dramatic results over recent years. Sports sponsorship has played a large part in increasing brand visibility, notably the high profile collaboration with Chelsea Football Club. In 2005, the brand became the club's official sponsor in a five-year partnership that marked the premiership giant's biggest ever sponsorship deal, and the second largest by Samsung, after its sponsorship of the Olympic Games. Samsung has aligned its brand with the

success of Chelsea who have accrued no fewer than six major trophies in the last three years. Samsung's strong sporting affiliations are global; it owns the professional soccer club, Suwon Samsung Bluewings, and the South Korean baseball team, Samsung Lions, in addition to sponsoring rugby league team the Sydney Roosters in the Australian National Rugby League.

Sport, and football in particular, remains an important way for Samsung to tap into and reach its target audience. The 2006 World Cup was a key milestone with the brand building a marketing campaign for the very successful R7 range of LCD TVs around one of sport's most high profile sporting events. The R7/R8 series are now the LCD TV of choice for the UK and Europe (Source: GfK).

Samsung's successful transition from an analogue driven product line to a cutting-edge and award-winning digital innovator

has seen it become the world's number one manufacturer of CDMA mobile phones, LCD monitors, DRAM memory chips and TVs. With a brand value of US$16.2 billion, Samsung Electronics was recognised as one of the world's top 20 brands by BusinessWeek magazine in 2006.

The last 12 months alone have seen the brand's efforts rewarded with more than 100 Samsung products receiving the industry's most influential design awards – the best ever annual showing for the brand. The prestigious International Forum Design (iF) organisation bestowed 28 iF design awards on Samsung products in 2007, more than doubling the number accrued in 2005.

The foundations of the Samsung brand are built around its core values of technology, design and innovation. In addition to providing premium products, Samsung is continually looking towards new ways of increasing brand awareness in order to maintain its position as a leader in digital technology and consumer electronics.

San Miguel
The Spanish
conquest

San Miguel's colourful history can be traced back to the Philippines. To be more precise, a district of Manila named San Miguel from which the fledgling company took its name.

At the end of the nineteenth century, a group of Spanish pioneers were inspired by a group of Spanish monks, that they found in the town of San Miguel, brewing beer. They used traditional time honoured methods, which created a desirable and distinctive tasting beer. Taking the knowledge of the monks back to their native Spain, these early entrepreneurs started brewing their own beer, which they named San Miguel in homage to their mentors.

May 1957 saw the launch of San Miguel in mainland Spain; from this point onwards the brand really began to expand. Thanks to sustained investment in technology and innovation (and the start-up of a number of breweries covering every region of Spain) the growth in the consumption of San Miguel steadily increased. Plans to continue its expansion into overseas markets such as the UK, Italy, Portugal, Sweden, France and Germany have been helped by the brand's integrity and considerable corporate support.

From the outset the founders wanted to remain true to the company's three defining principles: the brewing of a special quality beer, distribution throughout Spain and an ambition to export, both in the short and medium term. These fundamental ideals remain integral to the brand today.

Since 1967 San Miguel has been the leading Spanish beer export, with more than 700,000 hectolitres consumed in Europe and the Mediterranean area each year. The brand's presence abroad has grown steadily. In the UK, San Miguel is currently available on draught in 1,949 regional free outlets. It is also available in retail outlets, including Tesco.

A big part of San Miguel's marketing strategy in the UK comes through television campaigns. Its latest, Three Ships, which was first aired in July 2007, centres around the idea that San Miguel is the sign of a curious individual. It features a group of friends with the one who is noticeably more inquisitive than the others duly rewarded with San Miguel. The action takes place in the typically Spanish city of Seville, reinforcing the brand's Spanish heritage. The new campaign marks a shift towards a more sociable brand association, the idea of 'looking forward, beyond boundaries' which consumer research suggests resonates more with the brand's target market – 'bright young things' aged between 25 and 34. The campaign has already had a noticeable effect on brand recognition and

consumer engagement and will be reinforced later in 2007 by an experiential campaign in London, again focused around the idea that San Miguel is the sign of a curious individual.

In 2007 San Miguel commemorates the 50th anniversary of its commercial history in Spain. Today the brand forms part of the Mahou-San Miguel Group, the leading Spanish-owned beer-making concern. As the undisputed leader in Spanish beer exports, San Miguel represents over 70 per cent of Spanish brands, maintaining a high presence in more than 35 countries worldwide.

So what next? San Miguel is hoping to increase brand awareness through further high-profile television advertising, and to drive availability to ensure everyone can sit back with a San Miguel whether they are out and about or at home.

Please enjoy San Miguel responsibly.

Watch for three ships

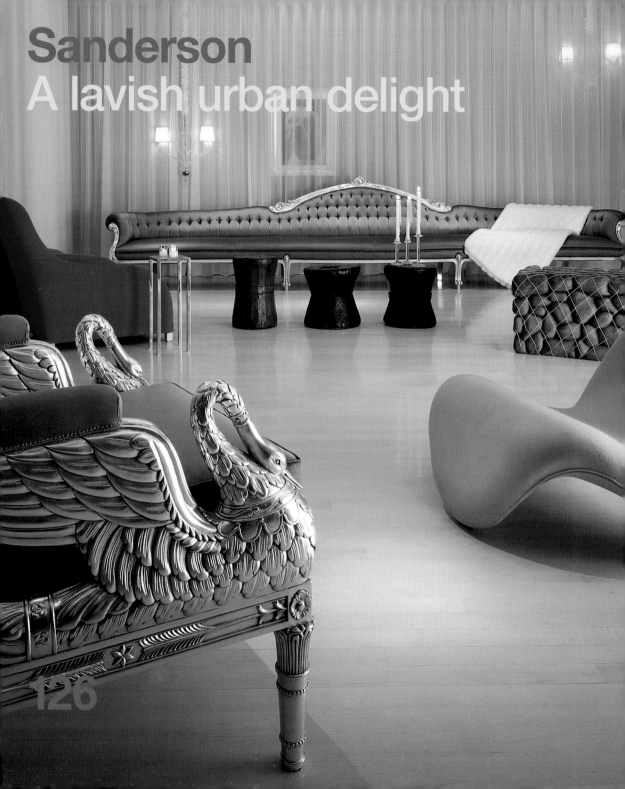

Sanderson
A lavish urban delight

morganshotelgroup.com

CoolBrands 2007/08

In a world where style is often mass-produced, Sanderson stands out for its bold use of experimentation and originality.

The mission behind the 150-room Sanderson – located in the heart of Soho, London's media and fashion capital – was to create the ultimate 'Urban Spa'; a retreat from the frenetic pace of the city. Visionary founder, Ian Schrager, initiated the collaboration between Morgans Hotel Group (credited with revolutionising the hospitality sector with the launch of the Boutique Hotel') and renowned French designer Philippe Starck, and in doing so introduced to the UK a modern hotel for the next millennium: radical, subversive and creative.

The hotel building – originally designed in 1958 as headquarters and showroom for the Sanderson fabric company – is a classic example of modern architecture that was ahead of its time. It is this archetypal design that lends the foundations for Sanderson's unusual room configurations: an indoor/outdoor Lobby with a private open-to-the-sky inner Courtyard and the notable absence of conventional walls.

Sanderson's floor-to-ceiling glass façade - used to diffuse and soften natural light - marked a new approach to the design and use of hotel public spaces; up until then entrances were typically dull and uninspiring. The imaginative combination of baroque and modern creates a lightly surreal landscape that alternates between extravagance and simplicity.

This eclecticism extends to the Long Bar - itself a work of art. The 80 foot long onyx rectangle glows with an integrated light and includes a tabletop overhang made from matte stainless steel. Starck

custom bar stools, with silver-leaf frames and white upholstered backs, feature an inset image of a woman's eye by photographer Ramak Fazel and complete the look.

Sanderson's in-house restaurant, Suka, serves authentic Malaysian cuisine, albeit with a European twist. Situated on the ground floor of the hotel, it has recently been redesigned by Paris-based architect and designer India Mahdavi and now encompasses the 'hidden' space following the Long Bar, as well as the whole of the Garden Terrace. The menu (created by New York chef Zak Pelaccio) is served in a typical Asian sharing style that reinforces its relaxed and casual surroundings, while retaining an inherent elegance synonymous with the brand. Fresh British and Malaysian produce are partnered with traditional French cooking techniques to create a range of dishes, from comforting home-style cooking to up-market luxury.

The feature that perhaps best captures the essence of Sanderson is its spa, Agua. Traversing two levels, and stretching over 10,000 square feet, it is the largest of all Morgans Hotel Group's spas and offers a range of up-to-date treatments and therapies within an ancient Roman style setting; mixing contemporary timelessness with the needs of modern urban life.

Innovative features and a meticulous attention to design detail throughout all of Sanderson's guest bedrooms challenge expectations of what a 'hotel room' should be. Spaces have been extended to create an open plan feel by removing inner walls, and features such as transparent glass bathrooms and electronically operated opaque silk curtains allow guests to develop both their own personal space and their own level of privacy. It's all part of the Sanderson ethos where structure and formal limits give way to a different personal environment aimed at inspiring individuality.

Sanderson epitomises the dawning of a 'new luxury', one that is smart, pared down, and tempered with a healthy dose of wit and irony: in essence a modern hotel with 21st century sex appeal.

Storm
Pioneering
individuality in
unlikely places

128

storm

In the past 20 years the fashion industry has globalised beyond recognition – along with the profiles of its leading players.

As a brand, Storm's strength lies in its unique ability to combine the artistic and commercial elements of fashion in a way that appeals to both the industry and the public, effectively acting as a bridge between business and consumer that few other brands manage to do successfully. Storm has consistently strived to set new industry standards, measured in terms of the achievements of its models and the brand evolution, while remaining a name that people can trust.

Storm's philosophy for its models has always been, like its founder's, to strive to attain the highest levels possible, providing the guidance to build long term careers based on talent and achievement. In a highly competitive environment where individuality and excellence are prized, the most successful models are those who offer something extra: Cindy Crawford, Ines Sastre, Eva Herzigova, Carla Bruni, Monica Bellucci, Carre Otis and Alek Wek are rightly acknowledged as stars whose talents reach beyond the camera's lens.

Storm was founded by Sarah Doukas over 20 years-ago, with financial backing from Virgin. It wasn't long before Storm became known for only taking on the best, and for discovering talent in unusual places. Sarah famously spotted the (then) 14 year-old Kate Moss while waiting for a plane at JFK airport. Just four years later Kate was contracted exclusively to Calvin Klein, an early landmark in a career that has set the standards to which other models now aspire. While Kate's achievements in the industry are legendary, it is the consistently superlative quality of her work that sets her apart, together with her uncanny ability to capture the mood of the moment in the way she dresses. Kate is the world's most admired style icon and she has opened a new chapter in her career by launching her first design collection, Kate Moss Topshop, thus combining her talent to create looks with her unrivalled experience in fashion. Together with her new 'kate by kate moss' fragrance, this new direction embodies the Storm philosophy.

In 2006 Storm expanded on this strategy, opening a Special Bookings division, which represents high-achievers from across the entertainment spectrum. Working with the existing management teams, Storm is bringing its strategic experience and strong commercial relationships to build credible brand partnerships. Clients include Emma Watson, Jaime Winstone, Peaches Geldof, Katherine Jenkins, Paolo Nutini and Rupert Everett.

A creative vision lies at the heart of Storm's approach and it was vision that enabled Sarah to recognise Kate Moss' potential all those years ago: today that vision remains the same. Discovered in Covent Garden by Storm, Lily Cole has gone from strength to strength, shooting top campaigns for Anna Sui, Hermes, Prada, Cacharel, Ghost and Moschino as well as working for Vogue in Italy, Germany and the US, and appearing twice on the cover of British Vogue. In tandem with her meteoric career, Lily has won a place at Cambridge University and has taken an active role in promoting environmental issues in fashion.

Storm is not afraid to take chances; finding models in unlikely places and signing unconventional talent – like Sophie Dahl at a time when she was larger than other catwalk models. Its emphasis on scouting for new talent by communicating directly with the public includes arranging competitions in conjunction with leading youth brands, such as Yahoo!, T4 and H&M.

Main image Photography by Ian Mckell. Additional images Photography by Sarah J Edwards (bottom left), Alastair Mclellan (bottom right)

Tanzania
The Land of Kilimanjaro and Zanzibar

Safari is the Swahili word for 'journey'; adopted internationally to describe an adventure into the wild, it is a fitting description given Tanzania's reputation as home of the safari.

It was in Tanzania's Olduvai Gorge, commonly referred to as the 'cradle of mankind', that Dr Louis Leakey discovered the fossilised remains of Homo habilis in the 1950s. The find was thought to be around one and three quarter million years-old and one of modern man's ancestors.

Around two thousand years ago Tanzania was a popular trading stop with Arab, Persian and Chinese merchants, with some eventually settling on the island of Zanzibar during the eighth century AD and setting up various trading routes inland including the infamous slave routes. The resulting crossover between the two cultures (the Arab settler and local tribes) led to the indigenous population of Tanzania today, living on the coast and the evolution of its own language – Kiswahili (Swahili).

Before the Arabs, Tanzania had been home to various African tribes over the years, most recently the Maasai from Kenya. The history and heritage of around 20 ethnic tribes contributes to its diverse cultural and historical make-up. The Cultural Tourism Programme, supported by SNV Netherlands and UNWTO, aims to give tourists a genuine cultural experience that combines nature, folklore, rituals, tales, art and ceremonies, touching on ancient customs and practices, many of which (such as coffee growing and production) remain today. Visitors can explore Tanzania's eight UNESCO World Heritage Sites with none

of the hardship but all of the adventure of its early pioneers.

With spectacular game viewing experiences in Tanzania widely regarded as some of the best in Africa, the country measures over 937,000 sq km. Its geographical position close to the Equator is flanked by other African states such as Kenya and Uganda in the north, the Democratic Republic of the Congo, Rwanda and Burundi in the west, and Zambia, Malawi and Mozambique in the south make it an ideal base for exploring central, eastern and southern Africa.

The Northern Tourist Circuit is probably the most developed of all Tanzania's tourist routes (although still remains unspoilt by over development) and includes many of the country's famous national parks such as the Serengeti, Arusha, Taranguire and Lake Manyara, as well as well-known landmarks such as the Ngorongoro Crater, the Olduvai Gorge and Africa's highest mountain, Mount Kilimanjaro. Rising above the plains at 19,344 feet, and with a diameter of 40 miles, Mount Kilimanjaro is the highest walkable summit in the world and Africa's tallest peak. It is also a dormant volcano, although not yet extinct.

Whereas the Northern Tourist Circuit may offer visitors the chance to see herds of wildebeest or flocks of pink flamingos emerging from the swirling mists of the alkaline lakes of Lake Natron, Manyara, Ngorongoro Crater and Momella – a sight believed to have given birth to the legend

of the phoenix – it is the Southern Tourist Circuit and game reserves of the south that truly capture the essence of the African adventure. The Mikumi flood plain, with its open grasslands, dominates the Mikumi National Park and offers opportunities to observe at close quarters lions, elephants, giraffes and zebra. The plain is also home to over 400 species of bird, many Eurasian migrants who stay between October and April. Other famous parks include Katavi, Ruaha and Udzungwa, all teeming with flora and fauna.

In addition to exhibiting at the major travel shows worldwide Tanzania hosts its own annual travel fair, which showcases over 200 exhibitors, covers a range of tourist enterprises and offers an ideal opportunity for overseas buyers and travel specialists to meet the market leaders in Tanzania's tourism industry and discover emerging projects and markets. In 2007, the fair attracted 5,000 travel trade professionals.

Tate Modern
Look again, think again

132

TATE

Housed in an imposing former power station on the bank of the River Thames, Tate Modern is home to some of the world's best-known modern and contemporary art.

Works by Picasso, Dali and Andy Warhol are exhibited in Tate Modern's Free Collection alongside current contemporary pieces, while recent special exhibitions have showcased the enduringly popular Gilbert & George as well as the Carsten Holler slides in the Turbine Hall. Tate was the first major gallery in the UK to brand itself and continues to lead the field internationally in arts communication: inviting, intelligent, though not overly academic, and challenging but never intimidating.

The brand was developed by Tate in partnership with Wolff Olins to coincide with Tate Modern's launch in 2000; the brief being to create a distinctive, worldwide brand that broadened the appeal of Tate's existing museums as well as Tate Modern and convey its forward-thinking approach to experiencing art. The brand's aim – to unify the Tate Collection at its four gallery sites – has increased visitor figures, from four to seven and a half million.

Tate Modern runs a number of campaigns each year. Although most are linked to the gallery's programme of exhibitions and events – by way of conventional high profile press and underground advertising – Tate Modern also experiments with more unusual techniques and strategies.

The brand's ongoing collaboration with advertising agency, Fallon, has produced a number of ground-breaking

campaigns such as the award-winning Tate Tracks, where high-profile bands like The Chemical Brothers, Klaxons, Union of Knives and The Long Blondes were invited to choose a piece of artwork in the gallery and compose a track inspired by it. The tracks were subsequently released (one per month) on headphones in the gallery beside the artwork – the only place worldwide where each track could be heard. Promotion for the campaign (aimed at attracting a new, younger audience) was through music channels, flyers outside gigs, blogs, Xfm, band fan sites and legal flyposting – all media that appeals to a young, urban crowd. Tate Tracks climaxes in Autumn 2007, with a competition on MySpace, to encourage members of the public to create their own tracks inspired by Tate artworks; the winner getting their track posted in the gallery.

Tate's brand values are imbued, not just through art, but also throughout every other aspect of the organisation. Its food subsidiary, Tate Catering, for example, aims to provide impeccably sourced and honestly priced produce, while Tate Modern Restaurant offers breathtaking views across London and a wine list chosen by sommelier Hamish Anderson. Tate Entertaining (its events company) runs both indoor and outdoor events that reinforce the brand mantra – open, inviting and fresh – and includes The Long Weekend, a four-day music

and art extravaganza that takes place over the May bank holiday each year.

The brand look emphasises Tate's approach. A simply written 'Tate' in upper case is modelled to provide a range of logos that reflect the fluidity and dynamic nature of the brand direction; the logo, inspired by the light on the top of Tate Modern, symbolises how a visit to Tate can be illuminating.

Tate has established a distinct brand appeal through its accessibility and a forward-thinking approach to art; a democratisation of gallery-going without the need to 'dumb down' and a shift of focus from art collections to the whole experience by putting people before art.

The Old Vic
Great plays, great performances and great nights out

134

The Old Vic has adopted a variety of guises throughout its history – from theatre for the nobility to a temperance music hall. Now it's back doing what it does best: producing thought-provoking plays, nurturing creative talent and bringing theatre to as wide an audience as possible.

The Old Vic's home has been a London landmark for over 200 years, having started life as the Royal Coburg in 1833 with the promise of an 'entirely new entertainment'. Since then the iconic building has played host to a range of productions starring leading actors of the stage – from Laurence Olivier's Hamlet to Ian McKellen's Widow Twankey. In 2004 Kevin Spacey was appointed artistic director of the newly-formed Old Vic Theatre Company, continuing the actor/manager tradition of Olivier, who led the National Theatre at The Old Vic in the 1960s and 1970s.

This reincarnation marked a new beginning for the Theatre, with more people than ever passing through its doors – testament to its imaginative programming and social entrepreneurship. The Old Vic's 2007/08 programme includes the world premiere of a new play based on Pedro Almodóvar's acclaimed film, 'All About My Mother'; the return of The Old Vic panto with Stephen Fry's witty new version of 'Cinderella'; Kevin Spacey in David Mamet's Hollywood satire, 'Speed-the-Plow'; and a double-bill of classic works directed by Sam Mendes for 'The Bridge

Project' – a unique three-year transatlantic collaboration between Mendes, The Old Vic and the Brooklyn Academy of Music in New York.

2006 marked the largest community initiative ever undertaken by The Old Vic. Working with the Imperial War Museum, a new play was commissioned to commemorate the 90th anniversary of the Battle of the Somme. The cast of 50 local residents and school children learnt new creative skills as they went from auditions to rehearsals and the final public performances at the Museum.

Innovative community projects such as these are an essential part of The Old Vic's aim to offer a range of learning opportunities to encourage new and diverse audiences. For the under 25s, £12 seats are available at each performance, reduced-price tickets are offered to Lambeth and Southwark residents throughout the year, and each production is partnered by a series of workshops aimed at giving young people the opportunity of working with established actors. The Old Vic presents the perfect hands-on environment for promoting and nurturing up-and-coming talent and offers help and guidance to young actors, directors, writers and producers taking their first steps in theatre through its New Voices Club. Members attend a series of year-round workshops and receive support for projects that they can then go on to develop with like-minded peers.

The 24 Hour Plays gala, staged annually at The Old Vic, helps to fund ongoing work with young people and the community. Over the course of just 24 hours, celebrated actors, writers and directors are challenged to create six short plays. It's the ultimate theatrical challenge, culminating in a unique evening of entertainment as the well-known faces test their talent in front of a

packed Old Vic auditorium. Previous participants have included Gael Garçia Bernal, Joseph Fiennes, Rufus Sewell, Michael Sheen, Meera Syal, Catherine Tate and Vince Vaughn.

Under the inspirational leadership of Kevin Spacey, The Old Vic is gaining strength as a theatre with the artistic vision to attract the best creative talent, produce memorable work and provide a great night out.

All photography by Ellis Parrinder

TomTom
Find your way
the easy way

Satellite navigation may have replaced drums as today's guiding light but the principle remains the same: helping people to find their way – which is where TomTom comes in.

Founded in Amsterdam in 1991 (originally as Palmtop) by graduates Peter-Frans Pauwels and Pieter Geelen, the brand is now the world's leading navigation solution provider, having sold more than 10 million all-in-one devices. The company changed its name from Palmtop to TomTom in 2001, with the arrival of Harold Goddijn as CEO. The name was chosen to denote the historic use of drums for navigation purposes with the distinctive brand logo that accompanied the new name – two playing hands – reinforcing this symbolism.

TomTom uses Global Positioning System (GPS) to send signals via satellites to GPS receivers. From these the devices can work out positioning, the required destination and how fast the user is travelling.

There is a TomTom to suit everyone's needs, from basic navigation to state-of-the-art feature rich devices. 2007 marked the start of a new era for the brand with several prominent launches. April saw the introduction of the TomTom ONE XL range, its features including a super-sized 4.3 inch high quality widescreen touch screen to provide drivers with an enhanced overview of the road and additional viewing information. Each device comes pre-installed with TomTom safety cameras, promoting the brand's ethos of safe driving and offering easy access to traffic update information through TomTom Traffic. Users also get

access to TomTom HOME, a free software application for managing, downloading, storing and transferring content from home computers on to a TomTom to keep the device completely up-to-date.

The TomTom community is growing daily with currently over two million TomTom HOME users.

Hot on the heels of the TomTom ONE XL came the launch, in June, of the TomTom GO range. Combining the brand's trademark stylish design with up-to-date technology, the range aims to give users the 'ultimate' driving experience. The host of features includes a unique and revolutionary new map technology, TomTom Map Share™, enabling drivers to update their map immediately and then share this with other TomTom users. The result: up-to-date maps, information and inside local knowledge at users' fingertips.

Safety is a key priority in the development of all TomTom products. The new TomTom GO Range comes with direct access to extensive safety and roadside assistance information. The 'Help Me!' menu, for example, includes information such as directions to the nearest hospital, car maintenance information and basic first aid instructions. A further safety feature, speech recognition allows the driver to input the destination address by simply saying the city, road and house number.

One of TomTom's most popular attributes is its ease of use; customers can fit devices straight from the box to their car or motorbike – making efficient

travel instant, stress free and safe. The brand's safety features (a component in all TomTom designs) were reinforced by the results of a recent independent study carried out by leading Dutch research institute, TNO. The key findings cited that satellite navigation devices improve a driver's behaviour in an unfamiliar area and destination, heighten alertness and reduce stress levels – all acknowledged to be contributing factors in road accidents.

TomTom continues to lead the fast growing market of satellite navigation and has won numerous consumer awards. TomTom drives innovation within the industry and is the world's most widely used and recognised personal navigation brand (Source: GfK).

Actually, fashionably late was never fashionable

TomTom are passionate about helping people get where they want to be quickly, safely and hassle-free.

There's a TomTom product to suit everyone's need. TomTom devices are available at John Lewis. For the latest product information visit in store or www.tomtom.com.

Find your way the easy way.

Triumph
Design classics
with engineering
passion

138

Founded in Coventry in 1887, The Triumph Cycle Company began producing powered cycles in 1902, the first simply named 'No 1'.

Over the next 18 years the company grew steadily, alongside its reputation for innovation, reliability and road-worthiness. In 1925 Triumph added automobile production to its expanding portfolio; by 1935 the motorcycle branch of the business was sold to Jack Sangster and renamed Triumph Engineering Company.

1937 proved a landmark year for Triumph, with the range of revamped singles (known as Tigers) and the 498cc Speed Twin, defining everything a modern motorcycle should be; the press raved, the public were intrigued and manufacturers inspired – the Speed Twin became an overnight success.

The two decades following World War II are referred to as the 'golden age' of British motorcycling with some of the world's best-known screen idols such as James Dean, Clint Eastwood, Steve McQueen and Marlon Brando, regularly appearing, both on and off celluloid, alongside their Triumph. The Triumph Bonneville – named after the record-breaking feats on the Bonneville Salt Flats by Johnny Allen – became an iconic symbol of that era and retains this cult status today.

A gradual slow down in production throughout the 1970s culminated in the liquidation of the company in 1983. It could have signalled the end for Triumph but instead John Bloor – the man behind the brand today – bought the intellectual property rights to the Triumph marque, paving the way for a modern approach.

In the subsequent 24 years, Triumph has helped kickstart a motorcycle revival both with those old enough to remember the golden age of bikes and a younger generation. Bloor remains a hands-on owner involved in the research, development, design and manufacturing side of the business, and has been helped in recent years by commercial director, Tue Mantoni. When an accidental factory fire temporarily halted production in 2002 Mantoni spearheaded a review of Triumph's commercial operations overseeing the repositioning of the brand globally. It now delivers consistent year-on-year growth and as production capacity grows, Triumph's range continues to evolve and diversify, from high-performance sports bikes and laid-back cruisers to retro-styled roadsters.

Although the Triumph range is divided into three distinct sectors – Urban Sports, Modern Classics and Cruisers – all of its motorcycles share several fundamental characteristics: each machine is powered by either parallel twin or in-line triple cylinder engines, which have a charismatic sound and distinctive feel; the designs are purposeful, blending form with function to deliver crafted machines with attention to detail and all have a well-balanced chassis with class-leading handling that makes Triumph products intuitive and easy to ride.

Personalisation remains an important aspect of motorcycle ownership and Triumph offers an extensive range of accessories and clothes – from the cosmetic to the functional. In 2005 Triumph collaborated with British designer Paul Smith on a range of branded clothing and two limited edition Triumph Bonnevilles, designed by Smith. The brand also joined forces with Umbro during the 2006 Football World Cup, as well as designer Patrick Cox to produce two machines to support a Virgin Unite charity event. Current projects include working with Factory Publishing on The Many World's of Jonas Moore concept; an innovative graphic novel for the iPod generation, aimed at increasing awareness amongst the future generation of motorcyclists.

Tyrrells
Farm reared gourmet chips

After 20 years of growing potatoes for supermarkets, William Chase hit upon the idea of turning his potatoes into the tastiest, hand-cooked gourmet potato chips.

In 2002, after travelling to America, William took the bold move of converting a potato shed on his farm in Herefordshire into a factory to make his first hand-cooked potato chips. Now, five years on, Tyrrells Potato Chips' are in the world's top food halls and the brand has evolved to become synonymous with artisan food.

Tyrrells grows older varieties of potatoes that are renowned for their flavour – such as Lady Rosetta, Record and Lady Claire - in the fields surrounding Tyrrells Court Farm. The company remains the only UK chip maker to grow its own potatoes and process them on the farm. No pesticides are used on the crop, and no artificial or GM products are used on the chips. Unlike other mass produced crisps, Tyrrells are produced in small batches and hand stirred using artisan methods. In fact it's not unusual for a potato to be dug in the morning and turned into chips by the afternoon.

The finest potatoes and root vegetables are individually inspected, washed and peeled before being thick-sliced into pure sunflower oil, retaining all their natural juices and goodness. While warm, the chips are delicately seasoned with specially created natural flavours.

In order to be as kind to the environment as possible, Tyrrells makes every effort to manage its carbon output through a variety of energy saving measures. The company grows all its own potatoes to keep food miles to a minimum, while

waste sunflower cooking oil is converted into bio-fuel on which delivery vehicles are run. A reed bed system filters the waste water from the factory before it is returned to the water table and waste vegetable peelings and chips are fed to local livestock.

The Tyrrells range now consists of 15 flavours – including provocatively packaged Naked Chips, classic Mature Cheddar & Chives as well as Ludlow Sausage & Wholegrain Mustard. Famed for creating original, imaginative new flavours, the seasonal flavour range includes Asparagus & Crushed Black Pepper and Summer Barbecue variants. In addition Tyrrells produces a range of vegetable chips, which includes mixed root vegetables, beetroot and honey glazed parsnips.

Complementing this is a range of dips including Caramelised Onion, Hot Red Pepper and Tomato & Sweet Chilli.

The range is continually evolving and Tyrrells Alternatives will shortly be on the market, which includes Habas Fritas – lightly spiced, cooked broad beans – and Chilli Rice Puffs. Plans are also underway for a Tyrrells Potato Vodka.

The brand hasn't gone unnoticed in its short history, receiving more than 40 major awards for product quality and

manufacturing standards. These include Small Business of the Year in the December 2004 Growing Business Awards; Midlands & East of England Entrepreneur of the Year, presented to Will Chase at the National Business Awards in 2005; and in 2006, Tyrrells was named New Exporter of the Year in the Food from Britain Awards.

Tyrrells has more than 5,000 customers in the UK made up of quality independent food retailers including Selfridges and Harvey Nichols as well as farm shops, delis, and gastropubs. It continues to deal directly with over 80 per cent of its customers – delivering straight from the farm gate to customers all over the UK – reducing 'food miles' and ensuring freshness.

Recently redesigned, the Tyrrells logo represents the company's farming roots. The addition of the leaf as an apostrophe signifies the rural values of Tyrrells and its support of family farms. Tyrrells has a passionate team behind it who tend every stage of process from seed to chip.

Vivienne Westwood

Rebellious style with a quintessential English twist

The British are admired worldwide for their individuality and Vivienne Westwood, the doyenne of UK fashion, epitomises this distinctive home-grown sartorial style.

It started back in 1971, when Westwood, along with her then partner Malcolm McLaren – who later went on to achieve further recognition through his association with leading punk band the Sex Pistols – set up shop in London's fashionable Kings Road. At that time London was leading the way in alternative youth culture and the Kings Road premises became a showcase for the label's original ideas and designs. During the early 1970s, as fashions and music began to change, Westwood adapted her shop, designs and surroundings to suit. The first shop name, Let It Rock – specialising in 1950s style clothing – became Too Fast To Live, Too Young To Die in 1972, with the design direction evolving more towards urban culture.

In 1974 Westwood once again changed the shop name to Sex, a deliberately provocative title that coincided with her dressing of controversial cult band, The New York Dolls. By the time the Sex Pistols hit the scene in 1976 – clad almost head-to-toe in Westwood creations – the shop's name had changed to Seditionaries, before its final reincarnation in 1979 as World's End.

As the 1980s dawned, Westwood unveiled her much awaited first runway collection, Pirate, marking a move away from street culture into the world of traditional tailoring techniques. In 1989 her creativity was formally recognised when John Fairchild, editor of Women's Wear Daily, declared her one of the six best designers in the world.

The following year was a seminal one for Westwood; her first menswear collection, Portrait, was launched in conjunction with Pitti Uomo in Florence. Furthermore, she was awarded British Designer of the Year, an accolade she went on to receive again in 1991. This recognition led to further industry honours; in 1992 Westwood became an Honorary Senior Fellow at the Royal College of Art and was awarded an OBE. Then, in 1993, she became Professor of Fashion at the Berliner Hochschule der Kunste in Germany.

Westwood's influence has shown no signs of abating in the 2000s. Her designs were irrevocably placed under the spotlight with a retrospective exhibition at the V&A in 2004 – the largest exhibition ever devoted to a British designer – celebrating her 34 years in the fashion industry. The retrospective opened during the Milan Fashion Week in the dramatic surroundings of Palazzo Reale.

In 2006, Westwood's contribution towards British fashion was officially recognised by the Queen when she was appointed a Dame.

Famed for attracting those with a rebellious spirit, Vivienne Westwood is a fashion label that transcends generations. Through an extensive distribution network the brand's products are today sold in 86 countries, with more than 10 different lines spread across five continents. These include: Gold Label – a 'demi couture' line and Westwood's most fashion-forward, innovative and recognisable collection; Man – for the fashion conscious man who appreciates an unconventional approach to classic designs; Red Label – for the enduringly elegant, timeless woman who wears designer clothes from day-to-day; and Anglomania – a youth-centric line that introduces Westwood's typical avant-garde passions to a new generation.

But in recent years it hasn't only been quirky British tailoring that has garnered Westwood praise; her range of fragrances that began with the launch of Boudoir in 1998, are also revered amongst fashion devotees. The latest perfume, 'Boudoir Sin Garden', was launched in May 2007 and in keeping with Westwood's signature style, it aims to be provocative, irreverent and stylish. This is followed in September by 'Let it Rock', the new fragrance.

Today Vivienne Westwood remains an independent company, with its eponymous founder recognised as one of the most influential fashion designers in the world today.

Yauatcha
An elegant, contemporary dim sum teahouse

Yauatcha offers value for money mid market dining – an all day grazing experience with modern, authentic dim sum and teas.

Founded by Alan Yau – the man behind Michelin starred restaurant, Hakkasan – Yauatcha was created to blend what he describes as the "fusion overdosed West with real far-Oriental cuisine". He took inspiration from the Chinese tradition of 'yum cha' – to have tea. The dim sum element has been introduced to this as the Chinese rules of hospitality dictate that drink shouldn't be served without food. The term has of late, come to refer to the social ritual of catching up with friends over dim sum.

Yauatcha opened in 2004 as London's first specialist all day dim sum restaurant and teahouse, providing a contemporary setting for eating, drinking tea and socialising, the traditional Chinese way.

Its founder's signature blend of high quality cuisine with cutting-edge design is immediately apparent. Situated on the ground floor and basement of Richard Rogers' Ingeni building in Soho, Yauatcha has – like Yau's two other London restaurants, Hakkasan and Busaba Eathai – been designed by Christian Liaigre. The two levels have contrasting ambience, from the light and airy ground floor teahouse with its white marble and full-height fish tank, to the cavern-like basement illuminated by electronic 'candles' and fibre optic 'stars', with glimpses of the kitchen behind a blue glass screen.

Yauatcha's menu is prepared under the supervision of head dim sum chef Soon Wah Cheong whose high standards have been recognised by influential industry bodies including the Michelin Guide, Zagat and The Tatler, as well as the Moët Restaurant Awards. It uses a 'core and peripheral' strategy offering 10 traditional dim sum dishes which form the core of this eating concept.

Yauatcha has modernised these 10 core dishes without compromising on quality and authenticity. Beyond this, Yauatcha experiments in creating the peripheral items in line with its product philosophy.

Yauatcha is currently working on developing its retail section of the teahouse with a range of tea scented candles, incense, soaps and china wear as well as chocolates, truffles, petit gateaux and patisseries. Specially designed packaging allows cakes and patisseries to be available as takeaway items. Indeed, Wallpaper* magazine recognised the cakes as the 'Best Snack' in 2005.

The first piece of china ware designed specifically for Yauatcha was a Japanese tea set by Shin Azumi, a renowned Japanese designer. Hsiao Fang, an accomplished Chinese potter then designed a series of Chinese tea sets. There are plans for Indian and English tea sets to follow, again designed by equally esteemed designers for Yauatcha.

Yauatcha's range of candles was launched in March 2007 after more than two years of development to perfect the scents, ingredients and design. They are made from completely natural beeswax, which ensures they are smokeless and paraffin free.

Yauatcha will be spreading the 'yum cha' word in 2007, with a further restaurant opening in Kuala Lumpur.

INNOVATION
STYLE
DESIRABILITY

CoolBrands 2007/08 – The Road to Cool

By Stephen Cheliotis Chairman of the CoolBrands Council

As chairman of the CoolBrands Council Stephen oversees the judging panel and selection process that determines which brands are awarded CoolBrand status; this article provides an overview of this rigorous process.

148

Background

The concept of CoolBrands came about in early 2001. The Superbrands organisation had at that time already been analysing the UK market for over five years to determine the nation's strongest consumer brands. The Superbrands that were identified certainly represented quality, reliability and distinction, however it was apparent that many other deserving, dynamic and interesting brands were being overlooked because the project invariably favoured the larger, more established mass market brands. That bias was fitting for the Superbrands programme but the organisation wanted to spread the net further afield and identify other brands that were also doing great work and so the CoolBrands concept began to take shape.

The aim was to seek out brands, large and small, established or new, that were deemed to be 'cool'. This invariably identified new brands and sectors, however a slight degree of overlap with Superbrands did occur.

At first Superbrands did not define what cool actually was, being that it is so subjective. The selection process merely asked the specially formed CoolBrands Council to consider whether they felt a brand was cool according to their own interpretation. In effect the organisation didn't define cool, but used the instinct of the Council who all had an insight into this area. The theory

behind this being that if a brand was immersed in interesting, exciting and cool products and/or services or marketing then those in the know would be advocates.

It soon became apparent that cool throws up a wide range of opinions and no two people will completely agree on what, who or where is cool. However Superbrands had the ability to provide a snapshot of opinion from qualified experts – equally this enabled the organisation to produce, off the back of the opinions of the Council, a publication full of case studies that provided fascinating, insightful and often inspirational reading. Move on six years and CoolBrands has become a high profile barometer of which brands have attained cool status, which now incorporates a consumer vote, tapping into the views of the UK public.

Over the years Superbrands has continued to refine the project, not only introducing the consumer vote but also conducting further research into the notion of cool. As a result benchmarks have been introduced to define what a CoolBrand is. Although cool is still personal and highly subjective, Superbrands has established the common factors and characteristics that people of varying ages and backgrounds consider to be inherent within a brand that is deemed to be cool. These have been defined as six features, highlighted above right. These drive the voting process and are considered by both the

1. **Style**
2. **Innovation**
3. **Originality**
4. **Authenticity**
5. **Desirability**
6. **Uniqueness**

CoolBrands Council and consumers, who take part in the YouGov vote.

The Selection Process

Each year, at the start of the selection process, Superbrands needs to ensure that the way in which the CoolBrands are determined is as wide reaching and thorough as possible and that the list is not influenced by commercial considerations. Therefore, unlike many other 'award schemes' that exist in the media and marketing industry, brands do not apply to be considered for CoolBrand status. Instead, Superbrands surveys the whole market knowing that the results will be both comprehensive and accurate.

The first stage of the process each year involves independent researchers creating a population list of the brands operating in the UK; these are gathered from various databases, magazines, blogs, websites, research reports, etc. Practically every sector is considered, from food to cars and fashion to electronics. The list is produced from scratch each year. Agencies and brands can suggest a brand for consideration but Superbrands finds that in nine out of 10 cases, the brand is already on the list. This is the case because the population list usually features well in excess of 5,000 brands and so few brands are missed.

To avoid commercial interests interfering in the process, the project is run entirely independently from the commercial team at Superbrands – the team that runs the associated CoolBrands membership scheme, which offers qualifying brands additional promotional and networking benefits for an annual fee. The result of separating the selection process and the membership scheme provides an entirely robust, transparent, and genuine conclusion. To the annoyance of the commercial team this results in many of its members, regardless of enthusiasm, failing to qualify for renewed membership the following year. In fact up to 40 per cent of Superbrands' clients in the CoolBrands project fall out of the rankings and therefore membership qualification.

Following this process, the population list is narrowed down to a short list – I work with independent researchers to do this – to establish a manageable sized list of brands for consideration by the CoolBrands Council. This year, the list featured just under 1,200 brands. Any brand considered a genuine contender is included; when there is debate about its credentials, a brand is given the benefit of the doubt so that the Council

can decide its fate. As a final check any Council member can request to include a brand that they feel has been omitted.

The 'short' list is then rated by each independent and voluntary Council member. I have continued to increase the size of the Council, from 21 members in 2006/07 to 27 members for 2007/08 (the current programme); this provides us with a diverse collection of perspectives and experiences. The big change in the Council this year is that we no longer have individuals from the marketing departments of brands that could feasibly qualify for CoolBrand status. This is to avoid an inaccurate conclusion that brand directors could have influenced their own brand's performance – in reality they were never allowed to vote for their own brand. Council members come from two fields: either they are media personalities that influence opinion and have to keep their fingers on the pulse of current trends, e.g. DJ Trevor Nelson or VOGUE.COM editor Dolly Jones; or they are senior figures from suitable marketing agencies, across a wide span of disciplines, e.g. Dylan Williams, the strategy director of ad agency Mother or Lee Farrant, a partner with brand experience company RPM.

The Council consists of a combination of new and existing members from the previous year; this ensures a balance between consistency and comparability with keeping things fresh and up-to-date.

Council members score each brand on the presented short list in their own time. They give each brand a rating from 1-10 based on their instinctive impression of the brand's cool status, but bearing in mind the six cool factors that I referred to earlier. Individuals do not research the brands or think too long about each entity.

Council members only consider a brand's status within the UK, although international strength may constitute part of a brand's make-up and improve its image. Individuals cannot score brands that they are involved with – i.e. clients of their company. In addition, competitor brands cannot be scored. Equally, Council members are asked not to score a brand that they are not familiar with – we do not want them to deduce a rating based on a glance at the brand's website or through second-hand opinion. In these instances an average score is applied to that brand based upon the ratings of the other Council members.

Council members score the brands in the context of the entire list, so there is no weighting by sector and they can allocate their scores as they choose. My commercial involvement with Superbrands is on a consultancy basis and I do not score the brands personally, again to avoid any 'commercial influence'.

The returned scores are collated and a league table is presented to the Council who have the opportunity to review and discuss it at a Council meeting. This is the final opportunity they have to add any missing brands, note any mistakes, examine the definition and the methodology and provide opinion on the next and final stage of the process, which is the consumer vote.

The top 50 per cent – this year 625 brands – according to the Council's scores are then put forward to the consumer vote, which is managed by the research agency YouGov. A total of 3,265 members of the public took part in the online poll.

Following that public vote a combined league table is produced, based on a weighted total score. Seventy per cent of this score is determined by the Council's rating, with the remaining 30 per cent coming from the consumer vote. This weighting is different to that of Superbrands programmes, where the consumer score forms 100 per cent of the final total and where the Council acts more as a filter. The reason for this is that whilst consumers ultimately decide the fate or success of a brand, it was felt that in the space of cool the opinion of leaders and influencers is vital as their awareness

of cool brands, particularly before they hit the mass market, is more developed.

The top 500 brands based on this weighted final league table are deemed to be those who qualify for CoolBrands status. All the brands featured in this publication are therefore in that top 500. As the project moves forward I am sure the process, and more importantly the brands that make the grade, will continue to evolve. We welcome your feedback and thoughts.

stephen.cheliotis@superbrands.uk.com

The myth	The truth
Brands pay to be considered for the CoolBrands programme.	All brands with the potential to succeed are considered. There is no cost to the brands.
Brands pay to be a CoolBrand.	All brands in the top 500 are CoolBrands regardless of any wider involvement with the Superbrands organisation.
The Council determines which brands are CoolBrands.	The Council plays an important role by approving and ranking the initial short list. However, the final top 500 is determined by a combination of their views and those of the UK public.
If you are a member of the current programme you qualify for next year's programme.	Each year the process starts afresh and brands are considered by the Council and members of the UK public. Only brands highly rated that year can take up membership and feature in the CoolBrands publication. Qualification one year is no guarantee of qualification the following year.

YouGov – Pioneering Research in to UK Public Opinion

YouGov, founded in May 2000 by Nadhim Zahawi and Stephan Shakespeare, is an online research agency pioneering the use of the internet and information technology to collect higher quality, in-depth data for market research and public consultation.

152

YouGov was one of the first companies to use online polling to register responses and opinions on topical issues such as crime, immigration and politics – as opposed to more traditional market research, which revolves around consumer and financial issues. It was this emphasis on topicality and opinion research that distinguished it from its online competitors and played a key part in raising its public profile during the formative years, as managing director, Panos Manolopoulos, explains.

"The core of the business initially was political polls, asking how people felt about politicians and the political issues of the day and also feedback from the public on how satisfied they were with services, for example, from the local council."

YouGov respondents were recruited, as with any other panel, from a broad spectrum of the UK's socio-economic make-up. While the company remit started off as fairly narrow, centering around the academic community, in 2001, thanks to its accurate predictions

of voting intention in the run up to that year's general election, it all changed.

YouGov's predictions – more accurate than any other poll – not only proved its online business model worked, it also put the company name firmly on the media map.

"The political response rates were high," says Panos, "because the survey worked in terms of engagement; when people really think through their answers they give you a considered response".

A further sign of YouGov's growing credibility gathering momentum came when it replaced Gallop as The Daily Telegraph's official pollster; its remit now extends far beyond the initial political agenda. YouGov is the UK's most accurate public opinion pollster; dominating Britain's media polling. It is also one of the most quoted agencies in Britain with a well-documented and published track record illustrating the success of its survey methods and quality of its client service work. An analysis reported in the Economist in October 2003 found that YouGov findings received more coverage in the media than any other pollster.

This expansion into other sectors (primarily media, technology and consumer) has been driving the growth of YouGov for the past four years – aided by sustained media representation and high visibility. In the political polling world a further seven elections have

**Panos Manolopoulos
Managing Director**

YouGov

taken place since 2000, with YouGov accurately predicting – within one percentage point – every outcome.

Following its accurate election and voting forecasting, YouGov received media attention somewhat disproportionate to the size of the business at that time; the publicity alerting relevant PR agencies (whose interest was to promote campaigns and work they do for the media) to YouGov's increasingly impressive track record in providing effective, independent online polling and thereby its potential as a credible associate partner who would produce accurate results and quality data.

According to Panos the increased volume of work YouGov started to pick up as a result of its growing kudos became an extension of the work it was already covering.

"From the strict topical issues YouGov started doing a variety of work for agencies whose end clients came from the private sector and also stared venturing into consumer-orientated work."

Panos, who has an 18-year track record in market research, is responsible for the business development strategy and research operations in the UK that support the organic growth of the business. Before joining YouGov his roles included senior positions at NOP World Limited, Taylor Nelson Sofres plc, and Lightspeed Research Limited, the online research agency of WPP Group plc – working for a wide range of blue-chip clients across survey methods. As a member of the Market Research Society and European Society for Opinion and Marketing Research, and with a BSc(Econ) from the London School of Economics, Panos is a regular speaker at industry conferences and seminars.

YouGov has worked with the Superbrands organisation over the past few years in providing comprehensive data that reflects the opinions of consumers.

"Superbrands approached us by virtue of the growing brand awareness of YouGov," explains Panos. "They wanted to work alongside a research supplier who could present independence, credibility and accuracy of the primary research to their audience in order to support the election of brands to CoolBrand status."

"We received the list of 625 brands to find out what the consumers think. This list of brands has been arrived at though independent research, followed by the CoolBrands Council vote."

The process that took place to select 2007/08's leading CoolBrands was conducted (in accordance with YouGov's core business model) using an online interview system, with brands organised into categories by sectors. Online research has been proved to be more engaging and stimulating than other interviewing techniques; it is not, for instance, seen to be as intrusive as questionnaires and is completed by invitation only, with YouGov pro-actively recruiting respondents from all age ranges, socio-economic groups and regions of the UK. The sample for each survey is carefully selected to ensure that it is representative either of the adult population as a whole or the specific audience that the survey is designed to measure.

This list was then presented to a nationally representative sample of 3,265 adults over the age of 18 – the process of selection mirroring the one YouGov uses for established political polls. In order to ensure that responses given were considered and respondents didn't become too fatigued, the selected list of around 625 brands was divided into four subsets; each then presented to 500 people. When all the results had been collated the percentage of people selecting each brand was ranked to form the CoolBrand's Top 500.

"By amalgamating it into statistical data tabulation format, responses were added together into the aggregate total resulting in a unified brand list," explains Panos. "The answers of individuals are then combined to see how each brand has performed."

"The way we match up the sublist of the brands with the subsets of demographically matched people is totally random to ensure a properly representative selection. Superbrands gave us a draft questionnaire with parameters and then it was YouGov's responsibility to hone that into a workable questionnaire that worked online and didn't contain any leading questions. Obviously we wanted to keep some continuity for comparison with the work we've done in the past and continue to measure similar attributes. As a client, Superbrands respected our expertise; allowing us to design the research methodology."

The successes of YouGov, securing its position at the leading-edge of the market research industry, have been recognised by a number of prestigious awards, not only those judged by industry professionals but also awards voted for by a wider public, reflecting both YouGov's strong professional standing and broader reputation.

One of YouGov's biggest product launches has been Brand Index, which measures consumer perceptions across 1,100 brands on a daily basis. This extensive and continuous level of polling is only achievable because of the quality of the research available online – it would not be feasible (or produce reliable data) to undertake a project of this scale using traditional interviewing techniques. The company's clients have diversified as the business has expanded; YouGov now works across a range of different sectors and industries including: a contractual agreement with The Sunday Times; work for the Association of British Insurers; an annual quarterly tracking programme of research that investigates and looks at the state of the nation in savings and pensions, the findings of which are included into the Government's annual report on savings and pensions each November; and a variety of work on the consumer side such as tracking work for Costa, PNO, uSwitch, BT, Oracle and Microsoft®.

YouGov recently expanded its business internationally both in the US and, one of the world's most exciting growth markets, the Middle East. Its decision to acquire a majority stake in an operation in Dubai reflects a strategic decision to seek specific opportunities for international expansion, rather than attempt, for the time being, to build a global panel. YouGov will continue to survey its US panel; otherwise, where YouGov is commissioned to conduct multi-national studies, it will continue to collaborate

with companies that have established online panels in the relevant countries.

As a relatively young company using new methods, YouGov has had to demonstrate its accuracy, which it has done repeatedly in events ranging from national, regional and party elections to the first Pop Idol contest – where it defied conventional wisdom by predicting that Will Young would win, and by what percentage.

Despite rapid continued growth and international expansion YouGov's core mission remains unchanged: continually developing new and pioneering ways to explore and understand public thinking.

www.yougov.com

Qualifying CoolBrands

2007/08

3
42 The Calls
7 For All Mankind
A Bathing Ape
A Butcher of
    Distinction
Abel & Cole
Abercrombie & Fitch
Absolut
Acqua Di Parma
Adidas
AGA
Agent Provocateur
Agnès B
Alexander McQueen
Alfa Romeo
Amazon
American Apparel
AmEx Red
Anna Sui
Another
Anya Hindmarch
Apple
Aprilia
Argentina
Art Review
Asahi
Aston Martin
Audi
Australia
Aveda
Azzedine Alaia
B&B Italia
Babington House
Baglioni
Bahamas
Balenciaga
Bali
Bang & Olufsen
Barbican Centre
Barbour
Bath Spa Hotel
Bebo
Beck's
Belstaff
Ben & Jerry's
Bench
Benefit
Bentley
Berghaus
Berkeley Hotel & Spa
Bermuda

Beyond The Valley
Biba
Bibendum
Billabong
Birkenstock
Blackberry
Blaupunkt
Bliss
Blogger
BMW
Bobby Brown
Bodyglove
Bolivia
Bollinger
Bombay Sapphire
Bose
Bottega Veneta
Boxfresh
Brabantia
Brazil
Breitling
British Airways
    London Eye
BSA
Buddhistpunk
Budweiser Budvar
Bugatti
Bulthaup
Bumble & Bumble
Burberry
Burton Snowboards
Burt's Bees
Cambodia
Cambridge Audio
Canon
Carhartt
Carluccio's
Cath Kidston
Central Saint Martins
Chanel
Charlotte Street Hotel
Chile
China
Chloé
Christian Lacroix
Christian Louboutin
Cirque du Soleil
Cobra Beer
Coco de Mer
Comme des Garçons
Converse All Stars
Courvoisier

Coutts & Co
Covent Garden Hotel
Crazy Bear
Crème de la Mer
Croatia
Cuba
D Squared
Daily Candy
Dazed & Confused
Dead Sea Spa Magik
Decléor
De'Longhi
Denon
Dermalogica
Design Museum
Designers Guild
Diane von Furstenberg
Didsbury Hotel
Diesel
Dior
Diptyque
Divertimenti
Dolby
Dolce & Gabanna
Dom Perignon
Dorset Cereals
Dr.Hauschka
Dr Sebagh
Dries Van Noten
Dualit
Ducati
Duchy Originals
EA
Earl Jeans
eBay
Eden Project
Egg
Eidos Games
Electric Cinema
Elemis
Elle
Emilio Pucci
Emirates
Emporio Armani
Etnies
Eurostar
Eve Lom
Evian
Expedia.co.uk
Farrow and Ball
Fender
Fendi

Ferrari
Fiji
First Direct
Flickr
France
Fred Perry
Fresh & Wild
Frieze
Gaggenau
Gaggia
Gap
Gaydar.co.uk
Gibson Guitar
Giles Deacon
Glenfiddich
Global Knives
Goldsmiths, University
    of London
Google
Gordon Ramsay
GQ
Grazia
Great Eastern Hotel
Green & Black's
Grey Goose
Gü
Guardian
Gucci
Guerlain
Guinness
H&M
Häagen-Dazs
Habitat
Hackney Empire
Hakkasan
Harman Kardon
Harper's Bazaar
Harvey Nichols
Havaianas
Heal's
Helly Hansen
Hennessy
Hermès
Hip Hotels
Hoegaarden
Hotel Chocolat
Hotel du Vin
Howies
Hugo Boss
ICA
I-D
Illy

India
Indonesia
Innocent
iPhone
iPod
Issey Miyake
Italy
iTunes
IWC
J Sheekey
Jack Daniel's
Jaguar
Japan
Jean Paul Gaultier
Jelly Belly
Jimmy Choo
Jo Malone
Jose Cuervo
Kenya
Kérastase
Kiehl's
Kirin
KitchenAid
Korg
Korres
Krispy Kreme Donuts
Krug
Krups
La Perla
La Prairie
Lamborghini
Land Rover
L'Artisan Parfumeur
L'Atelier de Joel
    Robuchon
Laura Mercier
Laurent Perrier
Lavazza
Le Caprice
Le Creuset
Le Gavroche
Le Manoir aux
    Quat Saisons
Leffe
Leica
Levi's
Liberty
Ligne Roset
Linda Farrow Vintage
Linn
L'Occitane
Loewe

Logitech
Lomo
London College
of Fashion
London Guildhall
Lonely Planet
Longines
Louis Roederer
Cristal Champagne
Louis Vuitton
Love Kylie
Lovefilm.com
Luella
Lulu Guiness
M&S Simply Food
M.A.C
Maglite
Magma
Malaysia
Maldives
Malmaison
Mandarin Hotels
Mandarina Duck
Manolo Blahnik
Marc Jacobs
Marmalade
Marmite
Marni
Marshall
Marvel Comics
Masai Barefoot
Technology
Maseratti
Mason Pearson
Matthew Williamson
McLaren
Mean Fiddler
Mercedes-Benz
Mexico
Miele
Mini
Missoni
Miu Miu
Molton Brown
Mongoose
Mont Blanc
Moog
MOP
Morocco
Motorola
Mozambique
Mr & Mrs Smith

Muddy Fox
Muji
Mulbury
My By Myla
MySpace
Napster
Nars
Neal's Yard
Neff
Net-A-Porter
New Balance
New Covent
Garden Food Co
New York Bagel
Company
New Zealand
Nicole Farhi
Nike
Nikon
Nintendo
NME
Nobu
Nokia
Notting Hill
Arts Club
Nylon
O2
Oakley
Ocado
Olympus
O'Neill
Orange
Origins
Panasonic
Paperchase
Parker & Farr
Patrick Cox
Patisserie Valerie
Paul & Joe
Paul Smith
Peroni Nastro Azzurro
Peru
Philosophy
Phyto
Piaggio
Pimm's
PJ Smoothies
Planet Organic
Play.com
Playstation
Poggenpohl
Pomegreat

Pop
Pop Bitch
Porsche
PPQ
Prada
Preen
Prescriptives
Prestige
Proenza Schouler
Proud Galleries
Puma
Purves & Purves
Quiksilver
Rachel's Organic
Range Rover
Reiss
REN
Rickenbacker
Rigby & Peller
Rip Curl
Riva Boats
Rizla
Roberts Radio
ROC
Roland
Roland Mouret
Rolex
Rolls Royce
Rothschild Wines
Rough Guides
Roundhouse
Royal Academy of
Dramatic Art
Rubik's Cube
S. Pellegrino
Saatchi Gallery
Samsung
San Miguel
Sanderson
Scalextric
Scrabble
Second Life
Seeds of Change
Selfridges
Sennheiser
Shaker
Shiseido
SKII
Skype
Smart Car
Smeg
Smiths of Smithfield

Smythson of
Bond Street
Snow+Rock
Soho Hotel
Somerset House
Sonia Rykiel
Sony
Sony Ericsson
Sophia Kokosalaki
Soul Jazz Records
South Africa
Space NK
Spain
Square Pie
Sri Lanka
St John
Staropramen
Steinberg & Tolkein
Stella McCartney
Stephen Webster
Stila
Stokke
Stolichnaya
Storm
Stussy
Sunseeker
Tag Heuer
Tanner & Kroll
Tanqueray
Tanzania
Tate Modern
Tattinger
Technics
Temperley
Thailand
The Conran Shop
The Cow Shed
The Dispensary
The Duffer of
St George
The Fat Duck
The Gaucho Grill
The Halkin Hotel
The Independent
The Ivy
The Lowry
The North Face
The Observer
The Old Vic
The Organic Pharmacy
The Photographer's
Gallery

The Pineal Eye
The Sanctuary
The Sunday Times
The Waterside Inn
Theo Fennell
Tiger Beer
Time Out
Tom Ford
TomTom
Top Trumps
Topshop
Trailfinders
Traveller
Triple Five Soul
Triumph
TVR
Tyrrells
Urban Decay
Urban Golf
Urban Outfitters
V V Rouleaux
Vanity Fair
Vans
Vera Wang
Vespa
Veuve Clicquot
Victoria's Secret
Vietnam
Viktor & Rolf
Villeroy & Bosch
Virgin Atlantic
Vitra
Vivienne Westwood
Vodafone
Vogue
Volkswagen
Wallpaper*
Wharfedale
Whole Earth
Xbox
Y3
Yauatcha
YMC
YouTube
Zara
Zetter
Zildjan

Cool Brand Behaviour
By Ralph Ardill
Founder & CEO
The Brand Experience
Consultancy

CoolBrands Council member Ralph Ardill shares some thoughts and observations on what it will take for cool brands to survive and thrive in tomorrow's brandscape.

The Brand Experience Consultancy brings together an exciting fusion of cutting-edge brand strategy, change management and creative consulting to provide board level advice on how brands can best explore and realise their full potential in the Experience Economy. The focus of the consultancy's work is built around unearthing powerful Organising Thoughts for its clients' brands which epitomise their core purpose and which are then brought to life to drive accelerated, holistic and highly impactful programmes of internal and external transformational change embracing people, products, places and promotions.

As a CoolBrand Council member for several years and as someone who spends most of their time repositioning, reinventing or revitalising brands, I'm often asked to comment on what we can learn from the annual CoolBrands list and of course, what is the secret of CoolBrand success.

Well, unfortunately there's no 'secret' or 'magic formula' but over the years I have de-coded a number of CoolBrand Behaviours that I believe are highly developed and revered within organisations that are capable of achieving sustainable CoolBrand status and success.

So let's take a look at eight of my current favourite CoolBrand Behaviours:

1. CoolBrands will be keeping it real

The balance of power between brands and consumers is shifting in our favour and with the wide-spread rise and mobilisation of consumer pressure groups, along with the increasing popularity of TV and press consumer 'watchdogs', we now have more ability then ever before to 'investigate' the attitudes, activities and actions that brands take behind-the-scenes in keeping these promises.

As a result brands will be looking to develop much stronger values-driven cultures to define, maintain and protect their integrity, which in turn will become an increasingly important dimension

Rough Guides
Keeping it real

of their external dialogue with consumers as they strive to earn our trust and engender loyalty by stronger communication and demonstration of their wider beliefs, values and commitments.

This 'reality-check' for branding is also likely to fuel the rise of more 'authentic' brands with increasing focus on the quality, origins and traceability of real ingredients, the skill of the real designers and craftsmen, more tangible demonstration and proof of reliable, consistent product/service delivery as well as more focus on the warm, genuine nature of the real people who sell, deliver and service them for us.

2. CoolBrands will be telling us stories

With the act of 'communicating' no longer any guarantee that a brand message has been received or understood, it's the age-old art of storytelling that is becoming a driving-force in the way brands will engage with us.

The focus being on the powerful articulation of brand stories – often built around real consumer and corporate characters and situations – that will draw us in to create brand content we will want to read and, like all of the best stories, want to recount and pass on to others.

An approach where captivating characters, plot and narrative become more important than the traditional obsession with audiences, messages and media.

Furthermore, where brands increasingly see themselves less as the editors, producers and broadcasters of one-way, pre-determined communication and more the seekers and source of captivating brand stories that are more openly shared with their internal and external brand communities.

3. CoolBrands will be making things simpler

We live in a 'surplus' society. We're spoilt for choice in terms of the products and services available to us, bombarded by thousands of messages daily and have attention spans that are diminishing as we demand more instant gratification from the things we buy and the wider world around us.

We're also recognising that time is one of our most precious resources and are increasingly looking for brands to make things simpler for us.

The pursuit of brand simplicity will not only relate to the creation of products that are easier and more intuitive to use and understand but will also become a wider organisational 'ethos' that

Gü
Telling us stories

Diptease?

We don't believe anyone can resist dipping their fruity bits in our new hot chocolate fondü. Made with 53% cocoa chocolate, served in a seductive black ceramic dish. If that's not enough, we're also offering ü the chance to win a naughty night in a five star hotel with a special friend. So, why not instantly see if ü have won at www.gupuds.com

TomTom
Making things simpler

extends across the brand value-chain to simplify the total relationships we have with brands.

From the development of products that are simpler to compare, find, buy and use through to plain-speaking contracts, terms and conditions, advertising, packaging and labelling.

Indeed the simplification of the total brand-customer relationship is set to become one of the most highly valued and differentiating points-of-difference amongst brands we highly appreciate and admire.

4. CoolBrands will be changing our lives

Our traditional pillars of society – state, religion, politics, community and the family – are all increasingly being questioned, tested and re-defined.

At the same time, with most of our basic human needs for food, shelter etc, now satisfied we will increasingly turn to brands to help us fulfil our more complex human needs to belong, feel connected, transform ourselves and experience true happiness and fulfilment in our lives.

In doing so brands will increasingly look to position themselves as the providers of transformational products, services and experiences that are no longer only 'consumed' but that also empower and inspire us with new knowledge, tools, and skills to help us improve the quality of our lives, whilst changing and improving ourselves in the process.

Whether this be helping us to become stronger, more intelligent, healthier, more fashionable, more informed, more attractive, more confident or simply believe we're now ready to put up those shelves.

Fresh & Wild
Changing our lives

5. CoolBrands will be feeling the difference

For decades brand owners have wrestled with the desire to 'humanise' the things we buy by giving them 'names', 'personalities', 'attitudes' and 'images' but often at the expense of conveying any true sense of emotion around the brand.

As brands increasingly recognise that it is emotions that drive most, if not all of our decisions they will begin to focus more effort on 'emotionalising' their entire approach to branding to help change our attitudes and behaviours and in turn build deeper relationships and engender our loyalty.

Agent Provocateur
Feeling the difference

An approach that will increasingly bring the passion of an organisation and particularly its people centre-stage, that will relish the opportunity to harness the power of design in its widest sense to increase our aesthetic and multi-sensory appreciation of the total brand experience, and that will not only communicate with consumers but also 'collude' with us to co-create and customise the brand encounters we want.

The holy grail of this more emotional focus on branding becoming the creation of brands that 'fans' can literally desire, fall in love with, cannot live without and cannot wait to evangelise about.

Eden Project
Caring for our communities

6. CoolBrands will be caring for our communities

Our ambivalence towards conventional marketing 'hype' and our increasing distrust of big institutions and political 'spin' is fuelling our insistence for brands to operate within a much higher set of corporate, social and environmental ethics.

As a result brands will look to invest much more of their time and resources in activities and initiatives that enable, mobilise and nurture our communities of interest. These activities working at many levels from brands targeting global issues such as climate change and sweatshop labour, through to more local and social challenges such as obesity, responsible drinking and improving school facilities.

This renewed focus on community also helping transform the future marketing of brands from an intrusive model of communicating largely un-wanted messages to a more participative genre of marketing focused on engaging consumers with activities and communications that we actively want to seek out.

7. CoolBrands will be getting more experienced

Our service economy has recently started to become commoditised by a more evolved experience economy where brands are going far beyond the basic provision of products and services to develop and 'stage' much more immersive, entertaining, enjoyable,

Nokia
Getting more experienced

memorable and higher value experiences for consumers.

Starbucks' transition of the humble coffee bean from a raw commodity bean into a cult coffee empire probably being one of the most impressive demonstrations of the business and branding possibilities that can be explored in the experience economy.

Going forward brands will increasingly look to create more powerful experiential products, services, places, communications and occasions that encourage consumers to want to spend more time and money with them.

This will also challenge brands to 'produce' these experiences whether they be in-store, outdoors, online or in-home in a much more holistic and multi-channel fashion to ensure that all operational, product, service and, perhaps most importantly, the human dimensions of these higher experiential promises are carefully orchestrated and consistently delivered.

3. CoolBrands will be daring to dream

Finally, as technology relentlessly drives our digital lives and as our personal information, knowledge, entertainment and communications increasingly become stored in 'cyberspace' and managed by computers, society – and in turn brands – will place new value on those human abilities and characteristics that cannot be digitised or automated.

Our myths, legends, stories, rituals, emotions, feelings, desires and dreams.

All will provide new inspiration as brands look to weave themselves into the fabric of our lives by capturing our imaginations, suspending our disbelief and providing new generations of products, services, experiences and spectacle that allow us to escape from the day-to-day and to explore our inner fantasies.

Products that move and mesmerise us, services that astonish and transform us, stories that fascinate and inspire us and experiences that immerse us in real or virtual worlds of possibility will all

become an important part of how brands will evolve.

An evolution where it is imagination not information that becomes the driving force as brands help us satisfy our highest human needs to belong and become all we can be whilst at the same time re-kindling our timeless appetite for adventure, exploration and the great beyond.

Tate Modern
Daring to dream

Brands Misbehaving

So there you have it, some thoughts, observations and predictions for the kinds of behaviour that the CoolBrands of today and tomorrow will be exhibiting.

That's not to say all CoolBrands exhibit all of these behaviours, or even that when they do so it's a conscious effort. Far from it and indeed it's the effortless ease with which CoolBrands achieve such engagement that fascinates us.

But going forward the pursuit of such behaviour is not only going to be the domain of CoolBrands and I believe all modern business will be increasingly challenged to come to terms with these ideas and behaviours, not so much in the interest of becoming a CoolBrand but to address the more fundamental questions of sustaining their ongoing survival, growth and prosperity.

Then again, as with many things in life, isn't it only a matter of time before the maverick misbehaviour of a minority becomes the mainstream behaviour of the masses?

So maybe its time for all mainstream brands and not just their CoolBrand counterparts to loosen-up and to start misbehaving a bit more.

ralph@thebrandexperienceconsultancy.com

Experience is Everything
By Lee Farrant
Partner, RPM

Experiential marketing explained by
CoolBrands Council member, Lee Farrant.

RPM was one of the first companies in the UK to recognise the power of Brand Experience. Such experiences lie at the core of the company's offering and RPM believes that experiential marketing is the only true form of marketing communication, everything else being just presentation.

RPM creates experiential marketing campaigns and events, connecting consumers in a creative and compelling way.

Clients include Apple, BSkyB, Cadbury, Diageo, The ECB, The FA, TFL, Scottish and Newcastle, UMBRO and Unilever.

What is experiential marketing or brand experience? This seems to be a common question we find ourselves faced with, despite the rising importance of the discipline within marketing circles. Generally, it is defined as live events where consumers interact 'face-to-face' either directly or physically with a brand, product or service. And, despite claims to the contrary, it's something that has been around for many years. In 1800 Winchester Rifles embarked on a frontier roadshow that allowed people to get to grips with its guns before parting with their cash; in the 1930s Henry Ford introduced the concept of taking people for test-drives in his cars. Both of these can be argued to be early experiential techniques.

So, why all the fuss now? With the proliferation and segmentation of media and a society that has become increasingly cynical towards traditional advertising and marketing techniques, experiential offers brands a way to reach their consumers directly in a credible and compelling manner. In recent surveys consumers have reported that experiential marketing allows for more in-depth product interaction, is more influential (particularly in the purchasing decision) and more engaging than any other form of marketing. In short, it is the most effective marketing discipline in driving purchase.

The key to a successful experience is to engage with the consumer when they are at their most receptive, i.e. when they

have chosen to experience your brand, not when they are having it foisted upon them in the shape of a 30-second commercial or full-page advert – interaction not interruption marketing. By giving consumers a tangible live experience at this point, it allows you to "prove the truth behind the brand claim". Essentially, you are creating an environment where people can discover for themselves that your brand tastes better, washes whiter, downloads quicker or really does want to make a difference. One of experiential marketing's greatest strengths is that it engages on a personal level and allows the consumer to create a real understanding of the brand's core message and values – by comparison all other marketing disciplines, although vitally important, are merely presentation tools. This type of interaction gives consumers the wherewithal to make an informed decision on their own terms as opposed to having someone else's view forced upon them.

The importance of this was highlighted in a recent article in The Sunday Times by restaurant critic AA Gill, who asked "where have all the critics gone?" In doing so he underlined one of the problems that people have with modern media… can they really trust what they read to be impartial? If a journalist is being taken out and wined and dined by a record label/film company/PR agent/motor manufacturer etc, is their summation of a product really going to be unbiased? Or is it simply a way of ensuring they're on the next jolly?

Journalists are often scared of upsetting companies, and this plays perfectly into the hands of experiential marketing. A live brand interaction allows consumers to bypass the unreliability of the opinions of others and cut straight to the product or service and let it speak for itself, in the process creating emotional connections that are deeper and longer lasting than those that can be achieved with traditional marketing techniques.

Another key factor in the discipline's rise is its media neutrality. It doesn't have to fit into any given page size or TV slot, in fact it is only limited by the brand or agency's imagination and budget. The skill comes in recognising where a live experience fits best into the campaign or customer journey. This is done by looking at the product, its lifecycle and the mix of media already in existence.

When properly integrated, a live element can add value to any marketing campaign. But it is important to realise that experiential marketing is not an alternative to other forms of marketing, it is a complement. There is a need to allow for and create dialogue with the customer, and the most effective campaigns create this opportunity in advance of the live aspect through techniques such as DM and digital, and continue it via CRM (customer relationship management) long after the event, thus building a stronger bond between consumer and product. As such, experiential marketing is now a 'must have' part of an integrated marketing plan, and no longer considered an 'option, alternative or bolt on'.

Taking a wider society view it could be said that experience itself is a new social currency. It's no longer simply the car you drive or the clothes you wear that define your character and status, it's where you've been and what you've done – in short your experiences – that make you the person you are. In that respect, experiential marketing could be said to be riding the crest of a social wave, and campaigns that tap in to this, by giving consumers an experience that they can take away for themselves, can be extremely powerful.

For example if, at a food event, you have a chef creating imaginative dishes that the consumer can then go home and demonstrate to their friends and family, you're instantly creating a strong tie with your product. Some of the best

experiential campaigns are the most simple – concentrate on giving the consumer easy wins and you've quickly got yourself a brand advocate.

In an age of increasing Corporate Social Responsibility, experiential marketing also provides an opportunity for brands to communicate openly and honestly on what they stand for. There is no more direct way to address or instigate a brand recovery, address barriers to market or challenge market misconceptions than by laying your brand bare in front of its critics or doubters – that is of course if you have the confidence in your brand to win through. So experiential not only has a vital part to play in marketing strategies but also within communication strategies.

So how are companies actually using experiential in the field? As marketing departments mature, people are growing to realise that it's not just direct sales that create sales. Audi, for example, uses a very soft sell approach because it is

onfident that once you've enjoyed the
udi experience you will buy into the
rand – the same could be said for Land
over. Go off and enjoy the Land Rover
xperience, spend time driving the
orld's best known 4x4 around a taxing
ff-road course and you'll never want to
ut your loved ones in the back of
nything else – despite environmental
hallenges. These experiences are about
uilding a compelling personal story as
o why you should own the product, and
's something traditional advertising just
annot do.

ome of the most effective experiential
ampaigns of recent times include the
ike 10k Run London event and Red
ull Flugtag. These events epitomise
erfectly the excellence of those brands.
ed Bull Flugtag says it all: Red Bull
oes indeed give you wings. The event
 a powerful, irreverent and funny
tatement. Here is a company that

manufactures one brand and their
sponsorship and experiences reflect
perfectly their maverick nature. So Red
Bull is associated with sports such as
Formula One, extreme mountain biking
and windsurfing, placing it as a cool
brand associated with cool sports.

With the Nike 10k, the brand has
adopted the same principle. It doesn't
associate itself with any of the big
marathons nor is it the sponsor of FIFA,
UEFA or any other big sporting event.
Instead, its events live and breathe its
brand statement… 'Just Do It'. They
don't want to be seen as the official
brand of anything, instead they position
themselves as the brand of the people
by putting on events that anyone can
join in – a sort of jumpers for goal posts
mentality. With Nike 10k, you don't have
to train for a whole year to compete and
the company sets up shop in various
parks around the city for three months
beforehand, offering people the
opportunity to swap their trainers for
Nike gear to try out.

What gives Nike its cool image is not
that it tells people it's cool, but that it
allows them to find out for themselves.
It says we make good product, we've
created a fun event, give it a go and
make up your own mind. This highlights
the changing nature of cool in marketing
terms; traditionally brand marketers
and their agencies dictated what was
cool and what was not. Now the onus
is on brand advocacy and brand
ambassadors, and experience is a key
driver in advocacy.

The role of the brand ambassador or
advocate is to make the consumer
believe that the people they consider to
be cool, or see as key opinion formers,
have gone out and spent their own
money on the product. One sports
industry professional claims the secret to
their strategy of advocacy is: "To have a
brand ambassador in a corner of Soho
House 'seeding' the latest kit to targeted
'industry movers', so it is profiled
alongside them in the upcoming music
and fashion press."

Over 2,500 years ago, Confucius said:
"Tell me and I will listen, show me and I
will remember, involve me and I will
understand." If he were around today,
maybe he'd add, "Give me the
experience and I will become a brand
advocate".

lee.farrant@rpmltd.com

The Geek to Chic of Tech Brands

By Nicolas Roope
Founding Partner
Poke London

Nicolas, a CoolBrands Council member, is also founder of boutique electronics brand Hulger. Here, he discusses the challenges facing technology brands.

Brands are having to spend more of their time digitally. Whether they like it or not.

People are touching, feeling and interacting with brands in new ways in new environments. Poke helps companies to use these new spaces and situations to develop products, services, communications and relationships. Ultimately evolving brands so they're as fluent in bits and bytes as they are in atoms.

The nerd archetype is always a bit of a techie. Tech is almost by definition not cool. Cool is drinking beer, doing drugs and burning your homework to the delight of attractive leather-clad onlookers. Tech is staying in because you're too spotty and socially inept to hang out and because there's too much maths homework to conquer. In fact why hang out at all, "it's illogical".

Technology brands are, by definition, disadvantaged so to achieve cool status at all is a minor miracle. Even mega fashion brands afford the dalliances of short run productions, statements and talk pieces that maintain their high status, whilst in tech-land minimum production numbers run into hundreds of thousands. As investment rises, so does risk and with risk, brands soon lose their appetite for adventure. They then anchor in the safe waters of mediocrity and the elusive and volatile cool disappears in a whisper.

Tech's achilles heel is the contradiction at the heart of its being. As a close cousin of science it is in the bloodline of logic, the binary building blocks that gel all these complex systems, pipes, bits and bytes together into an intuitive narrative. If you make a radio it has to work and its functions must be apparent and easy to use. But cool isn't about logic or what you get when you boil everything down to constituent parts, instead it bubbles off idiosyncrasy and emphatic individualism, the guy who makes his own rules versus the one who learnt them from a book or worse, a teacher.

So how can you make something that works and performs a desired function, that is usable and practical, and yet has that easy air of that rare desirable distinction?

Floating to the surface of the grand meritocracy of brands are a handful of technology companies that aren't led by logic and yet still manage to provide the user with the functions they desire. The difference is that they aren't defined by function, rather something more elusive, grander, something almost holy. If the CoolBrands book existed 25 years ago Bang & Olufsen would have been in there for sure. This was when I met my first B&O at my uncle's beach house in Denmark. Sleek, long and low, it had no discernable knobs or controllers, just subtle dips and grooves as cues for magician like interventions, a hand passing over to control volume, causing previously hidden hairline LEDs to expose themselves only to softly dim back behind the hard dark gloss façade. The form, materials and interaction with these devices were unnecessary or even absurd, yet the poetry of these elegant operations invoked previously unknown dimensions of desire, an experience almost erotic in nature. B&O were making much more than music centres, they were making shrines to contemporary culture, (and Jean Michel Jarre) objects which elevated us from the humdrum to the hip. These manifestations of a richer philosophy than we'd been previously accustomed to still echo through technology today, particularly in mobile phone design where the hard definitions of buttons and borders are melting into blobs and blocks that look like polished semi-precious stones. Interaction design draws from the same language of smooth gestures of scrolls and soft-touch screens compared to the ploddy point and click inputs of recent times.

B&O are still on our list today, still guarding and evolving a rock solid brand in an industry rife with quick sand. The few brands that keep hold of cool never allow themselves to be compared or commodified, always staying out of the reach of their competitors who might have all the same buttons but none of the soul. Leica, also on our list, shares many of these attributes, its confidence and precision deeply apparent in every turn and hard-edged furrow of these weighty, handsome machines. Even the shutter mechanics seem to sing a song of artfulness. This isn't just taking pictures.

Some technology brands have an easier access to coolness. Like fizzy drinks that win favour with fickle teenagers by associating with flavour-of-the-month-pop-princesses, tech brands are sometimes lucky enough to get some beneficial rub off from things already centre stage. The R&D department of Marshall still need dorky doctorates from Imperial to finesse the circuits in these rock boxes, but because these amps have sat on stage behind just about every music-making legend over past decades they have secured the brand a god like status.

The right place at the right time still stands for a lot. Technology that mediates music has this advantage over tasks like satellite navigation (although TomTom made it into the top 500, well done!). Sennheiser, because the music connoisseur broadcasts their choice wherever they're brandishing their oversized cans. Bose, with their branded boxes in every sleek bar and club and more recently adorning every boutique hotel suit from New York to Knysner. DJs are cool and so are their tools, so Technics make it in again and are unlikely to exit until all the world's vinyl is melted down.

People's tendency to associate things is the marketeer's key tool of persuasion. For camera brands, the connection to fashion is their low hanging fruit. The "gdssser gdssser gdssser" of motor-winds on high stress fashion shoots have long established the Nikons, Canons and Olympuses (all in the list) as names which share the limelight with supermodels and glossy feature spreads. Hard-edged front line documentary imagery too relates these names back to us, black beaten Canons in the hands of "are they courageous or crazy" photographers against the backdrop of war torn grainy Vietnam.

Associations with music, fashion and the front line have woven a heritage for these brands that provide a platform, a right and a reason to exist and the genetics that ensure continual renewal and reinvention along the lines of their breeding. Heritage brands have a gravity that buffers short-lived falls from favour. They become reference points that are always fixed in the hearts and minds of the public so are always springboards for new thinking and new ideas, something that's very hard to synthesise. Heritage embodies authenticity, a cornerstone of cool.

But heritage alone is not enough to stay at the top. Great brands have frequently fallen from grace, toppled by their reluctance to reinvent or, in the case of tech, simply by being outmoded. The killer formula draws strength from heritage and from the fans and supporters loyal to their cause but uses this to amplify new ideas that respond to the times and to the new landscape of technical possibility. Motorola made some of the first car radios and put the first radios in space and yet of late they're enjoying the spoils of the meteoric successes of the RazR that managed to appeal to both the adoring mainstream and the discerning, design aficionado. The same technical prowess applied against the same principles in a modern context ensured Motorola still came out on top.

Apple too has managed to continually reinvent itself successfully whilst always sticking close to its guns on issues of simplicity, materiality and formal elegance and the same integration of object and experience as the first Macintosh delivered over 20 years ago. The iPod's application of contemporary technologies and behaviours might betray the fact that it still has a lot in common with the company's principles. It is this continuity that gives Apple the right to innovate in the way that it does, throwing down radical alternatives to interaction that still somehow make a lot of sense to the user (the mouse back in the 1980s and more recently the iPod scroll wheel). Other brands wouldn't necessarily get consumer buy-in because these idiosyncratic interfaces would seem alien and impenetrable, whilst from Apple they are accepted as the expectation is there that they will thus be better to use – and for good reason. So powerful is this platform that Apple has created that the iPhone launch managed to generate the biggest product launch buzz so far this

millennium, so much so that people were already contemplating the form and function of the iPhone long before Apple had even announced it was going into production.

In addition to Apple finding the perfect balance between form, materiality and function, it has also managed to straddle two usually distinct worlds, trendsetters and the mainstream. Rarely do mainstream brands also hold favour with the in-crowd, but Apple miraculously manages it.

This ability to cross from cool to mainstream is also shared by a new breed of web centred brands, names like Google that are so ubiquitous and yet still have something special that puts them up there, slightly beyond mechanical

definition, something that makes them truly iconic. And strangely they have none of the visual styling or cues that would invite a definition of cool, but even this somehow increases the effect as the friendly cartoon logo is a clear sign it's not here to impress and we all know not trying makes you cool.

YouTube, Skype and MySpace also span the marketeers' hierarchy of opinion formation. These youthful, exuberant brands earn their status through creating cultures akin to the recreational social spaces of the physical world but in many ways have become bigger, better, truly multicultural and fully joined up experiences. Their atmosphere is a breath of fresh air set against formulaic and controlling broadcast channels and so they earn a place closer to the hearts of the participant.

As the web reaches total ubiquity, not only is it home to these rampant emerging brands but also an increasingly influential fabric of opinion formation and the maker and breaker of reputations. What would the iPhone have been without those billion conversations before its launch?

So technology brands, we might expect, will become more numerous in our list as years pass.

One could also conclude that, in a way, all brands to a greater or lesser extent, have an element of the techie about them...

nik@pokelondon.com

Start Creative

Great ideas are rare, yet it is ideas that differentiate organisations and create value. The best ideas are also born out of thinking and working together. For over a decade, pursuing this way of working has allowed Start to deliver inspiring creativity that meets business needs.

Founded in 1996 by Mike Curtis and Darren Whittingham, Start Creative is a cross media brand consultancy group based in Soho, London. It is now a top 10 independent agency in the UK with clients around the world.

Start's core proposition is 'ideas made well'. We're in the business of ideas and creativity, and we specialise in branding, brand marketing and digital media. Key to the success of our work is the relationship we have with our clients. We work closely with them to fully understand their business strategy and values, helping us to craft effective, creative solutions that are built to last.

What we do:

- Brand design: brand strategy and management, writing and tone of voice, identity design, brand environment, brand engagement

- Digital: website design, online advertising, iTV, mobile, multi-media, moving image

- Brand marketing: direct marketing, interactive marketing, loyalty, direct response

Who we do it for:

Clients include: Virgin, adidas, Bentley, Schroders, BBC, Royal Mail, Hilton, Hertz, thetrainline, COI, Alliance & Leicester and IoD amongst many others.

Our longest client relationship is with Virgin. We've worked on numerous projects for a whole host of group companies, including Virgin Media, Virgin Atlantic, Virgin Mobile and Virgin Trains. We also worked closely with Virgin Management to update and develop the master Virgin logo – the famous Virgin script – so it can go on expressing the brand's challenger spirit well into the future.

Contact:
Jonathan Cummings
jonathan@startcreative.co.uk
07802 749376

CoolBrands 2007/08 Cover Design

In creating the identity for CoolBrands 2007/08, Start developed three creative concepts that reflected the overall theme and the member brands.

From these three options, one was chosen by the CoolBrands team and developed into the identity you see on the cover of this book and below. Every member brand features in the hand drawn lettering of the logo.

The illustration was created by Si Scott, an artist with a unique style of hand inked and penned artwork blended with modern typography. Si has produced work for Hugo Boss, Volvo, Pentagram, Burton Snowboards, Miller, Nike, Boots, Orange, Marks & Spencer, MTV and Guinness amongst others. His work has been featured in major publications and exhibitions around the world.